S0-ADG-936

ALSO BY FRANCINE SEGAN

Movie Menus:
Recipes for Perfect Meals with Your Favorite Films

Shakespeare's Kitchen:
Renaissance Recipes for the Contemporary Cook

THE PHILOSOPHER'S KITCHEN

RANDOM HOUSE

NEW YORK

THE PHILOSOPHER'S KITCHEN

Recipes from Ancient Greece and Rome

for the Modern Cook

FRANCINE SEGAN

Photographs by Tim Turner

LIBRARY OF CONGRESS CATALOGING-IN-PUBLICATION DATA
Segan, Francine.
The philosopher's kitchen : recipes from ancient Greece and
Rome for the modern cook / Francine Segan.—1st ed.
p. cm.
Includes bibliographical references and index.
ISBN 1-4000-6099-0 (alk. paper)
1. Cookery, Greek. 2. Cookery, Roman. I. Title.

TX723.5.G8S43 2004
641.5938—dc22   2003061731

With love and gratitude to my mother,

ELEANOR ODDO,

for teaching me to cherish the past,

stay rooted in the moment,

and always look to the future

FOREWORD

The Philosopher's Kitchen offers an intriguing look at the customs and daily life of antiquity, of which food played an important and prominent role. Food, in every respect, was a consuming passion. In ancient times—along with emphasizing the importance of nourishing the mind—large, extravagant, bountiful gatherings were viewed as essential to nourishing community. Food was a way to connect with others. I was intrigued to learn in reading the delicious recipe for an appetizer of pureed olives mixed with herbs and spices that appears on page 5—a contribution from Cato—that the Roman statesman considered sharing a meal a way to create bonds between people, and called the dinner table "highly friend-making." Meals were also a means of expressing one's philosophy. Pythagoras, an outspoken vegetarian and accomplished cook, insisted that a nonmeat diet fostered physical and mental health and longevity. (Pythagoras's tasty Cucumber with Raisin-Coriander Vinaigrette on page 64 will silence his critics—at least while they partake of it— to this day.)

As chef at Molyvos, I have a great appreciation of and interest in the history of spices, flavor combinations, and cooking techniques. I was delighted to discover in these pages that many of my own Greek recipes that depend on unusual preparations of sweet ingredients with savory, or rely on unconventional uses of traditional items like coriander, dates, barley, and rue, have a precedent in recipes that are several thousand years old. Rediscovering the flavors of antiquity in these exciting and easy-to-make recipes connects one to the past and expands one's cooking repertoire.

As you peruse these pages I think you, too, will experience the astonishing and enchanting conjunction of past and present. *The Philosopher's Kitchen* will most surely inspire you to experiment in your kitchen with the time-honored flavors of classical cuisine. These exotic but simple recipes—updated and adapted to accommodate modern ingredients—will surely be featured prominently among the memorable and delectable meals you create for family and friends.

Kali oreksi,

Jim Botsacos
Molyvos, New York City

ACKNOWLEDGMENTS

Deepest thanks to the outstanding professionals at Random House—my extraordinary editor, Mary Bahr, Todd Doughty, publicist extraordinaire, Laura Ford, Shelley Berg, Anna McDonald, Pei Koay, Allison Saltzman, and Stacy Rockwood. I am forever indebted to Wes Martin, talented culinary professional, for so generously sharing his creativity in recipe development. Thanks to Tim Turner for his nonstop energy, insights, and enthusiasm, and for creating glorious photographs.

Heartfelt appreciation to Antiquarium Ltd., the renowned gallery in New York City, and to Joseph and Robin Coplin for so graciously permitting us to photograph their extraordinary antiquities. Thanks also to an anonymous collector for allowing us to photograph a unique antiquity. Warm appreciation to the wonderful New York Academy of Medicine Library and to the New York Public Library, two of Manhattan's treasures, for guidance and access to rare books and manuscripts.

Special thanks to Professor Zvi Yavetz, noted classicist, for providing sage scholarly advice and direction. Thank you especially, Dr. Yavetz, for the gift of Gellius.

Every recipe in this cookbook has been tested and retested to ensure that the results achieved in my kitchen can be duplicated. I am deeply indebted to the gourmet home cook recipe testers: Mary Misch, Hope and Warren Hagler, Fran Dichter, and especially Judy Borger, whose advice greatly enhanced many dishes.

Warmest appreciation to Paul and Lori Shields, Nach Waxman, Matt Sartwell, Elliot Brown, Judy Singer, A. J. Battifarino, Tina Ujlaki, John Vassilaros, Alexandra Gersten-Vassilaros, Bob Strassler, and Fannie Oddo for their wonderful input. Special thanks to Stephen Viscusi for planting the seed and encouraging me to write a food-related book.

One of the many joys of working on this project was discovering a world of incredibly giving and generous "foodies." Thank you all for sharing your expertise.

CONTENTS

INTRODUCTION

Philosophy, art, architecture, literature, astronomy, mathematics, medicine, psychology, political theory, and sports were all profoundly influenced by the ancient Greeks and Romans. Their legacy to our culture continues to affect our daily lives.

Customs such as flipping a coin to make a decision, the thumbs-up sign, putting candles on a birthday cake, sending a basket of fruit as a gift, and wearing a wedding ring on the third finger of the left hand all have roots in antiquity. Throwing a pinch of spilled salt over the shoulder, carrying a rabbit's foot for good luck, and making a wish on a chicken bone are just a few superstitions inherited from the ancients.

Many modern words and phrases come from ancient Greek and Latin, including *Achilles' heel*, *hermaphrodite*, and *Pandora's box*. Psychology especially has borrowed heavily, with terms such as *narcissism*, *the Oedipus complex*, *kleptomania*, *phobia*, and the *Pygmalion complex*, which were all derived from ancient Greek. The very word *psychology* comes from the Greek word *psyche*, breath of life.

The Olympic Games, the marathon, and ball sports all originated in Greece. The ancients' legacy includes the Mediterranean diet and many insights into medicine, health, and longevity from Hippocrates and others. It was Hippocrates who first noted the diagnostic value of interpreting a patient's dreams, and still today all physicians take the Hippocratic oath.

The teachings of philosophers such as Plato, Socrates, and Aristotle are so fundamental that we often quote them without even realizing it. It was Plato who said, "The life that is unexamined is not worth living," and Aristotle who coined "One swallow does not make a summer." Menander called "a spade a spade" in the fourth century B.C., and "having the Midas touch" comes from a Greek myth. Aesop gave us expressions such as "sour grapes," "Don't count your chickens before they hatch," "a wolf in sheep's clothing," and "Slow and steady wins the race."

Works by Homer, Euripides, Sophocles, Ovid, and Virgil continue to inspire modern novelists, playwrights, and moviemakers.

Roman architectural and engineering feats include still-standing aqueducts, arches, and buildings. Amphitheaters, such as the Colosseum, where tens of thousands viewed gladiator and mock sea battles continue to evoke awe. Ancient architecture has influenced countless modern neoclassic buildings around the world, and its design influences can be seen in homes, museums, parks, and even clothing. In fact, several black-and-white photographs in this book are of modern American design elements influenced by the past.

Democracy, which we so strongly identify with America, began in ancient Greece, and the term itself comes from the Greek *demos,* the people. Even the political filibuster arose in antiquity: Cato, who "did not wish to have the motion before the house carried," attempted to make a daylong speech until Caesar had him arrested.

It is the culinary legacy of the ancients that inspired this cookbook. Many delicacies found on a table in antiquity are still served today. Dishes such as pesto, custard, pasta, pizza, baklava, and pancakes all have their roots in ancient Greece and Rome. What sounds suspiciously like the first ham sandwich is even mentioned by the Greek playwright Aristophanes: "Fetch me the paunch of a suckling pig killed in the autumn, with some hot rolls." Numerous cooking techniques such as seasoning with wine and herbs, cross-cutting ham to bake it in a honey glaze, adding truffles to special dishes, and baking in a water bath all have their origins in antiquity.

I know nothing except the fact of my ignorance.
—SOCRATES, CIRCA 470—399 B.C.

Most of the cookbooks used by the ancient Greeks and Romans have been lost through the ages. In many cases all that remains are the titles mentioned in the writings of others, such as *Vegetables and Sicilian Cooking; Pickles; On Cakes; Gastronomy;* and *The Art of Dining.* However, I have drawn on many other sources for a sense of the types of foods eaten then:

- Artists' representations of daily life on Greek vases and drinking vessels, floor mosaics, and Roman frescoes
- Writings on food and health by physicians and philosophers such as Hippocrates, Galen, Plato, and Aristotle
- Books on farming by Cato the Elder and Varro
- Historical accounts written in antiquity by Gellius, Suetonius, Plutarch, Tacitus, and Pliny the Elder
- Literature, plays, and poems such as Marcus Martial's humorous epigrams, Petronius's the *Satyricon*, Homer's the *Iliad* and the *Odyssey*, and the plays of Aristophanes
- Personal correspondence and diaries of Cicero, Marcus Aurelius, and others
- Archaeological finds at sites such as Pompeii, Hadrian's villa at Tivoli, and Herculaneum

One of my favorite sources for recipes is *The Philosopher's Banquet*, a book on the foods, dining customs, and entertainments of ancient Greece written in the second century. The fifteen-volume work is structured as a series of dinner table discussions. Reading it made me feel as if I was eavesdropping on a Roman feast enjoyed by friends chatting about Greece's auspicious past.

Another important fund of information is the cookbook *De Re Coquinaria* (*On Cookery*), written in the first century. It is the oldest known surviving cookbook, and its 478 recipes provide a glimpse of the foods eaten by the ancient Romans and Greeks. Divided into chapters with such charming titles as "The Gardener," "The Gourmet," and "The Fisherman," *On Cookery* includes some recipes that might sound odd to our modern ears, such as stuffed dormice, roasted cow womb, and grilled rooster testicles. However, it also contains many dishes found in restaurants today, such as mussels in wine sauce and honey-roasted baked ham. Some ingredients used then are no longer available today, while others, such as truffles, oysters, and "the best virgin olive oil," are still prized by modern gourmets.

The past resonates in the present. Re-creating the cuisine of the ancient Greeks and Romans helps us connect in some small but wonderful way to their time, teachings, and lives.

THE
PHILOSOPHER'S
KITCHEN

NICANDER, writing in the second century B.C., notes
that the ancients typically began their meal with a
multidish appetizer: "The first platter, leading the main
courses, will contain a sea-urchin, some raw smoked
fish, capers, a wine-soaked bread, a slice of meat, and
a bulb in sour sauce."

This communal appetizer was often the topic of
humorous writings. One ancient Greek play described
a greedy character who gargled with and plunged his
hands into scalding hot water as training so he could be
the first guest able to grab up the steaming hot tidbits.

Chapter 1

AD GUSTUM: APPETIZERS

HERBED OLIVE PUREE

MINTED GARLIC SPREAD

CHICKPEA DIP WITH GRILLED PITA

SEARED SIRLOIN WITH LEMON-HERB CRÈME FRAÎCHE

SPAGHETTI WITH CARAMELIZED ONIONS

LAMB ON SKEWERS WITH MINT MARMALADE

RED LENTILS IN GARLIC-ROASTED ARTICHOKE BOTTOMS

ASPARAGUS FRITTATA

ALMOND MEATBALLS WITH DATE MUSTARD

MUSSELS IN CUMIN-SHERRY SAUCE

FREE-FORM CHERRY LASAGNA

ASSORTED FIG APPETIZERS

SMOKED TROUT CUSTARD WITH DILL

Clockwise from top: Minted Garlic Spread, Chickpea Dip with Grilled Pita, and Herbed Olive Puree

HERBED OLIVE PUREE
Serves 10

It is a hard matter, my fellow citizens,
to argue with the belly, since it has no ears.
—CATO THE ELDER, 234—149 B.C.

Cato, the Roman orator and statesman, wrote a book about small farm management in which he detailed a recipe for chopped olives mixed with herbs and spices eaten at the start of a meal. This modern version is not only wonderful as a dip with pita bread but also delicious tossed with cooked spaghetti.

$1/2$ cup pitted oil-cured black olives

$1/2$ cup pitted large green olives

$1/4$ cup chopped sweet onion

1 garlic clove, minced

10 fresh mint leaves

$1/4$ cup extra virgin olive oil

1 teaspoon fennel seeds

1 teaspoon ground cumin

1 teaspoon ground coriander

$1/4$ cup minced assorted fresh herbs, such as parsley, mint, and basil

6 pita breads, warmed and cut into quarters

1   Puree the olives, onion, garlic, mint leaves, oil, fennel seeds, cumin, and coriander in a food processor until smooth. Place the puree in a serving bowl, cover with plastic wrap, and set aside at room temperature for at least 6 hours.

2   Before serving, stir well, top with the minced herbs, and place on a plate with the warm pita bread sections.

ORIGINAL RECIPE

Green, black, or mixed olive relish to be made thus: Remove stones from green, black, or mixed olives, then prepare as follows: Chop them and add oil, vinegar, coriander, cumin, fennel, rue, mint. Cover with oil in an earthen dish, and serve.

—*ON AGRICULTURE*, CATO THE ELDER

OLIVES have been cultivated in the Mediterranean region since at least 2500 B.C.

According to legend, whichever god gave the people of Greece the most esteemed gift would earn the right to name their most important city.

Poseidon's gift, a waterway through the city, provided fresh drinking water and easy access to the Mediterranean. Athena gave them olive trees.

While the citizens were grateful to Poseidon, they preferred Athena's gift. Not only were the olives a long-lasting and delicious fruit on their own, but they also produced a useful oil. In return for the gift of olives, Athena was granted the right to name the city after herself, Athens.

The Parthenon, a temple that overlooks Athens, was built in Athena's honor.

MINTED GARLIC SPREAD

Serves 10

Mint was a symbol of hospitality, and even poor peasants serving simple fare honored their guests by rubbing platters with the herb. Here fresh mint pairs with tangy garlic to create a wonderful spread for assorted vegetables or as an accompaniment to grilled foods.

According to Greek mythology, mint was created when Hades, the god of the underworld, was caught flirting with a nymph. In a fit of jealous rage his wife, Persephone, turned the nymph, named Minthe, into the plant that now bears her name. Photograph on page 4.

3 cups cubed crusty bread, crusts on

3 tablespoons fruit vinegar

4 garlic cloves, minced

2 tablespoons honey

$\frac{1}{2}$ teaspoon ground coriander

$\frac{1}{2}$ teaspoon ground cumin

$\frac{1}{2}$ cup grated Parmesan cheese

$\frac{1}{2}$ cup extra virgin olive oil

Salt and freshly milled pepper

$\frac{1}{3}$ cup fresh mint leaves

Assorted raw vegetables for dipping

1 Place the bread cubes, vinegar, and $\frac{1}{2}$ cup of water in a food processor. Allow to stand until the bread has absorbed all the liquid, about 10 minutes.

2 Add the garlic, honey, coriander, cumin, and cheese. Puree until smooth. Slowly add the oil and continue to puree until incorporated. Season to taste with salt and pepper. Add the mint leaves and pulse a few times to incorporate. Serve in a bowl surrounded by raw vegetables

ORIGINAL RECIPE

Hollow out an Alexandrian loaf [bread from Alexandria, Egypt, often flavored with cumin], soak in water mixed with vinegar. Put in the mortar pepper, honey, mint, garlic, fresh coriander, salted cow's milk cheese, water, and oil. Cool in snow and serve.

— *ON COOKERY*, APICIUS

CHICKPEA DIP WITH GRILLED PITA

Serves 8

And gold chickpeas were growing on the banks.

—SAPPHO, CIRCA 610—580 B.C.

Sappho, referred to as the "tenth Muse," was often quoted in ancient literature. Unfortunately, only fragments of her poetry have survived. This dish is inspired by one such fragment and by the many delicious chickpea purees found on the island of Lesbos, Sappho's birthplace.

Alexis, the fourth-century B.C. playwright, joked, "How many traps to catch bread do unhappy mortals set," referring to the many dipping appetizers served before a Greek feast. This puree makes a wonderful "trap" for warm pita or flatbreads and is also delicious served on a bed of salad greens. Photograph on page 4.

1 large onion, diced

$\frac{1}{2}$ cup olive oil

1 cup dried chickpeas, soaked overnight, rinsed, and drained

1 teaspoon dried oregano

1 bay leaf

$\frac{1}{2}$ teaspoon freshly milled pepper

1 teaspoon salt

$1\frac{1}{2}$ cups vegetable or chicken stock

2 large garlic cloves, chopped

Juice and grated zest of 1 lemon

6 pita breads

3 tablespoons minced fresh mint

1   Sauté the onion in $\frac{1}{4}$ cup of the oil in a large saucepan over medium heat until golden, about 10 minutes. Add the chickpeas, oregano, bay leaf, pepper, salt, and stock. Bring to a boil. Lower the heat and simmer until the chickpeas are tender and the stock has been absorbed, about 1 hour. Allow to cool slightly. Discard the bay leaf.

2   Put the mixture in a food processor along with the garlic, lemon juice, and remaining
    $\frac{1}{4}$ cup of oil. Pulse until combined but still coarse. Place on a plate.
3   Preheat the grill or broiler. Grill or broil the pita breads until warm, about 1 minute per
    side. Cut into triangles and arrange them around the dip.
4   Serve the chickpea dip topped with the lemon zest and fresh mint.

SEARED SIRLOIN WITH LEMON-HERB CRÈME FRAÎCHE

Serves 6

*In writing of great men it is proper to record not only
their serious activities but also their diversions.*

—XENOPHON, CIRCA 431—352 B.C.

Xenophon, a contemporary and close friend of Socrates, wrote about the philosopher's everyday life. Xenophon recounted that Socrates enjoyed predinner exercise, rubdowns, and baths at one of Athens's many public gymnasiums. He described Socrates' lively dinner conversations with far-ranging topics such as the definition of good looks in a male, how money can take away one's freedom, and the benefits of wine. This dish is inspired by one such dinner conversation in which Socrates attempted to define greed in relation to the ratio of meat to bread that a man ate.

Enjoy this delectable seared sirloin thinly sliced and served with focaccia or your favorite bread.

4 teaspoons dried oregano

1 garlic clove, minced

1 tablespoon extra virgin olive oil

1 boneless sirloin, about $1\frac{1}{2}$ pounds

Salt and freshly milled pepper

$\frac{1}{2}$ cup crème fraîche

1 tablespoon whole milk

1 teaspoon grated lemon zest

2 teaspoons freshly squeezed lemon juice

1 teaspoon chopped fresh mint

$\frac{1}{2}$ recipe Etruscan Focaccia (page 189) or 1 loaf bakery-bought bread

1   Combine 3 teaspoons of the oregano, the garlic, and the oil in a small bowl. Season the meat with salt and pepper, and firmly press the oregano mixture on both sides. Set aside while you make the sauce.

2   Mix the crème fraîche, milk, lemon zest, lemon juice, mint, the remaining teaspoon of oregano, and $\frac{1}{2}$ teaspoon of salt in a small serving bowl. Cover and refrigerate until ready to use.

3   Heat a nonstick skillet over medium-high heat. Sear the meat until cooked to the desired doneness, about 4 minutes per side for medium. Transfer to a cutting board and allow to rest for 10 minutes before slicing.

4   To assemble, slice the meat across the grain into $\frac{1}{8}$-inch-thick slices. Slice the focaccia into 1-inch-thick slices and toast. Spread about $\frac{1}{2}$ teaspoon of the crème fraîche mixture on it and top with a slice or two of the steak. Serve immediately.

SPAGHETTI WITH CARAMELIZED ONIONS

Serves 6

Onions were thought to be aphrodisiacs, and both the ancient Greeks and Romans served them at wedding feasts to "seek the door of Venus."

In this modern version the onions are slow-cooked to create a creamy sauce without using either cheese or cream. Spaghetti tossed with this silky vegetarian sauce is topped with toasted bread crumbs and pine nuts, providing a lovely contrast of textures. The sauce can be made hours ahead and reheats nicely. Inexpensive yet elegant, this dish is perfect for a large group.

3 large sweet onions, thinly sliced

2 medium red onions, thinly sliced

1 teaspoon dried marjoram

1 teaspoon dried thyme

$\frac{1}{4}$ cup extra virgin olive oil

$\frac{1}{4}$ cup pine nuts

$\frac{1}{3}$ cup plain dried bread crumbs

$\frac{1}{2}$ cup white wine

1 tablespoon honey

1 tablespoon muscatel or sherry vinegar

Salt and freshly milled pepper

1 pound spaghetti

$\frac{1}{4}$ cup minced assorted fresh herbs, such as parsley, mint, and basil

1   Sauté the onions, marjoram, and thyme in the oil in a large skillet over low heat for at least 45 minutes, until very soft.

2   In the meantime, prepare the topping. Toast the pine nuts in a small, dry nonstick pan over medium heat until light golden. Reserve in a small bowl. Using the same nonstick pan, toast the bread crumbs over medium heat, stirring frequently, until they are golden brown. Add the bread crumbs to the toasted pine nuts and reserve.

3   Bring a large pot of salted water to a boil.

4   After the onions have cooked for 45 minutes, raise the temperature to high and caramelize them for 8 to 10 minutes. Add the wine and honey, and continue cooking on high until most of the wine has evaporated. Remove the onion mixture from the heat and stir in the vinegar. Season to taste with salt and pepper.

5　Drop the pasta into the boiling water and cook according to package directions, then drain. In a large bowl, toss the cooked spaghetti with the onion sauce and minced herbs. Top with the pine nut and bread crumb mixture and serve immediately.

THE ANCIENT Greeks and Romans did not have spaghetti as we know it. However, many ancient texts describe a very thin, dry sheet of dough cut into various shapes. This dry dough was fried or baked but not boiled. Boiling pasta in broth or wine did not occur until the Middle Ages. Interestingly, according to the *Oxford English Dictionary*, the word *macaroni* is derived from an ancient Greek word for barley cake, which hints at a relationship between the two.

LAMB ON SKEWERS
WITH MINT MARMALADE
Serves 8

This is one of more than one hundred sauce recipes for grilled meats listed by the Roman gourmet Apicius.

In antiquity, ingredients were ground in a mortar to use raw or to incorporate in sauces. Apicius used this grinding method so often that he is referred to as the "mortar chef."

You'll also love this delicious marmalade with grilled vegetables, fish, and chicken.

$1/4$ cup raspberry or other fruit vinegar

2 tablespoons golden raisins

4 pitted dates, minced

1 teaspoon honey

2 tablespoons pine nuts

2 tablespoons grated Parmesan cheese

1 cup fresh mint leaves

3 tablespoons extra virgin olive oil

Sixteen 1-inch cubes leg of lamb, about 1 pound

Salt and freshly milled pepper

8 small wooden skewers, soaked in water

1   Simmer the vinegar, raisins, dates, and honey in a small saucepan over medium heat until the raisins are soft, 2 to 3 minutes. Allow to cool to room temperature.

2   Puree this mixture, along with the pine nuts and cheese, in a food processor until smooth. Add the mint leaves and pulse until minced. Slowly add the oil and continue blending until smooth.

3   Toss the lamb cubes with half of the mint marmalade in a large bowl. Cover with plastic wrap and refrigerate for at least 1 hour and up to 12 hours. Put the remaining marmalade in a small serving bowl and season to taste with salt and pepper. Cover and refrigerate.

4   Preheat the grill or broiler. Liberally sprinkle the lamb with salt and pepper. Place 2 lamb cubes on each wooden skewer and grill or broil until the lamb reaches the desired doneness, about 1 minute per side for medium.

5   Serve with the reserved marmalade on the side.

ALTHOUGH there are many references in ancient writings to earlier cookbooks, the oldest surviving complete cookbook is attributed to a Roman named Apicius. It is a little difficult to sort through the true authorship, however, because there were many ancient gourmets with the last name Apicius and the book, *On Cookery*, is probably a compilation of recipes from many chefs.

Ancient historians recount fantastic tales about Apicius's quest for exotic and rare foods. He apparently spent huge sums on luxurious delicacies made with the highest-quality ingredients. According to one story, Apicius set sail for northern Africa in search of the then-famous crabs of Alexandria. As he approached Alexandria's shore, he spotted a fishing boat and requested a sample of its freshest catch. Unimpressed with the crabs, he asked for better. After being assured that these were the best to be had, Apicius turned around and made the long journey home without ever touching Alexandria's shore.

Legend has it that when his fortunes took a turn for the worse, Apicius killed himself, since he could no longer afford his culinary extravagances.

RED LENTILS IN GARLIC-ROASTED ARTICHOKE BOTTOMS

Serves 6

The ancients employed many dishes to whet the appetite.
—ATHENAEUS, CIRCA A.D. 200

Athenaeus, a Greek living in Rome in the third century, noted that the ancients often started a meal with a first course of assorted light appetizers such as pickled beets, mixed vegetables, delicate fish, and a variety of purees for dipping breads.

This Roman vegetarian appetizer makes a wonderful light start to a multicourse dinner party. If you prefer, substitute canned artichoke bottoms, since broiling them with the garlic-scented oil removes any slight tinny taste that canned foods can sometimes have.

1 large onion, diced
$\frac{1}{2}$ cup extra virgin olive oil
3 garlic cloves, minced
$\frac{1}{2}$ cup white wine
1 tablespoon honey
$1\frac{1}{2}$ cups vegetable stock
1 cup red lentils
1 bay leaf
1 teaspoon ground cumin
1 teaspoon ground coriander
Salt and freshly milled pepper
6 large artichoke bottoms, fully cooked
2 tablespoons minced fresh parsley or mint
2 tablespoons crumbled feta cheese

1   Sauté the onion in 2 tablespoons of the oil in a medium saucepan over low heat until translucent, about 10 minutes. Add two-thirds of the garlic and the wine and honey. Raise the heat and bring to a boil. Simmer until the wine is reduced by half, 3 to 4 minutes.

2   Add the stock, lentils, bay leaf, cumin, coriander, and ½ teaspoon of salt, and bring to a boil. Lower the heat and simmer for about 1 hour, or until the lentils are soft and all the liquid has been absorbed. Discard the bay leaf. Puree the lentils in a food processor with ¼ cup of the oil just until coarse. Season to taste with salt and pepper, and set aside.

3   Preheat the broiler.

4   Mix the remaining 2 tablespoons of oil with the remaining garlic. Brush this mixture on the cooked artichoke bottoms. Place them on a nonstick baking sheet and broil until golden, 1 to 2 minutes. Fill the center of the artichokes with the lentil puree and top with the minced herbs and cheese. Serve warm.

ASPARAGUS FRITTATA

Serves 4

Well done is quickly done.

—AUGUSTUS CAESAR, 63 B.C.—A.D. 14

Augustus Caesar, the first Roman emperor, coined the phrase "quicker than boiled asparagus," referring to any swift action. Historians claim he originated a number of other whimsical expressions, including "Let us be satisfied with *this*, Cato!"—meaning that we should make the most of the present rather than dwell on the past. Augustus, also known for his splendid dinner parties, was much admired for his talent at coaxing even shy guests into conversation.

Egg dishes were popular appetizers in antiquity, as we can infer from the Latin expression *"ab ovo usque ad malum,"* from egg to fruit, the equivalent of "from soup to nuts." This delicious asparagus frittata makes a perfect appetizer or, when served with a salad, an elegant light lunch.

6 large eggs

$\frac{1}{2}$ teaspoon ground coriander

$\frac{1}{2}$ teaspoon dried savory

2 tablespoons minced fresh parsley

Salt and freshly milled pepper

3 tablespoons olive oil

12 thin asparagus stalks, cut into 1-inch pieces

1 small red onion, minced

3 tablespoons crumbled feta cheese

2 tablespoons minced fresh chives

1 Beat the eggs, coriander, savory, and parsley in a bowl. Season to taste with salt and pepper. Set aside.

2 Heat the oil in a skillet over high heat. Add the asparagus and sauté until tender, about 4 minutes. Add the onion and continue cooking on high until golden, 3 to 4 minutes.

3 Lower the heat to medium, pour in the egg mixture, and scramble slightly to mix. Cook until just set and beginning to turn golden. Invert the frittata onto a greased flat plate and then slide it back into the pan to cook the other side until golden.

4 Top the frittata with the cheese and chives, cut into quarters, and serve warm.

ALMOND MEATBALLS WITH DATE MUSTARD

Serves 6

Live each day as though your last.

—MARCUS AURELIUS, A.D. 121—180

The ancient Romans ate reclining on couches in dining rooms lavishly decorated with mosaics, frescoes, and art objects. They even scattered rose petals on the floor before a feast.

The Romans, like the Greeks before them, did not use forks but ate elegantly with their fingers, following such etiquette nuances as picking up preserved fish with one finger but fresh fish with two. Foods such as these luscious bite-sized meatballs with date mustard would have been delicately eaten with the fingers of the right hand.

2 shallots, finely minced

2 tablespoons finely minced celery

6 dates, finely minced

2 tablespoons olive oil

1 teaspoon caraway seeds

2 tablespoons finely chopped blanched almonds

$\frac{1}{2}$ teaspoon salt

$\frac{1}{4}$ teaspoon freshly milled pepper

1 pound ground lamb

1 cup white wine

Pinch of ground nutmeg

1 teaspoon dry mustard

1 teaspoon yellow mustard seeds

2 tablespoons raspberry or fruit vinegar

1 tablespoon honey

1   Sauté the shallots, celery, and half of the dates in the oil in a small skillet over low heat for 3 to 4 minutes, or until the celery is tender. Allow to cool.

2 Combine the shallot-celery mixture with the caraway seeds, almonds, salt, pepper, and lamb in a small bowl, mixing well. Form into twenty-four 1-inch meatballs, cover, and refrigerate.

3 To make the date mustard, bring the wine, remaining dates, nutmeg, mustard, and mustard seeds to a boil in a small saucepan. Lower the heat and simmer until the wine is reduced by half, about 5 minutes. Allow to cool slightly, then put the wine mixture in a mini food processor and blend with the vinegar and honey.

4 To cook the meatballs, put them in a nonstick skillet over medium heat and sauté, turning once, until browned and cooked through, about 2 minutes. Or preheat the broiler and broil the meatballs on a nonstick baking sheet for about 2 minutes.

5 Serve the meatballs with toothpicks to dip into the date mustard or, if you prefer, toss the meatballs in the mustard, skewer with toothpicks, and arrange on a serving platter.

ORIGINAL RECIPE

Sauce for tidbits. Pepper, celery seed, caraway, savory, saffron, shallots, toasted almonds, Jericho dates, liquamen [fermented fish sauce], oil, and a little mustard; color with reduced must [reduced pulp after the wine grapes are mashed].

—*ON COOKERY*, APICIUS

FOOD that fell to the floor during a meal was believed to belong to the gods, and it was considered bad luck to sweep it up during dinner. The ancient Romans even decorated their dining room floors with mosaics depicting realistic-looking scraps of fallen food.

MUSSELS IN CUMIN-SHERRY SAUCE

Serves 4

I was surprised at how similar this two-thousand-year-old recipe is to the modern classic French dish, mussels in wine sauce. While modern-day recipes call for dry white wine, this called for "sweet raisin wine," which is similar to our sherry. The other slight variation is the addition of cumin, a spice popular with the ancient Romans that adds a lovely fragrance to this delicate appetizer.

2 tablespoons extra virgin olive oil

1 large leek, white and tender green parts, thinly sliced

2 garlic cloves, minced

$\frac{1}{2}$ cup sweet sherry

$\frac{1}{2}$ cup fish stock

$\frac{1}{2}$ teaspoon ground cumin

4 pounds mussels, in shells, scrubbed and debearded

Salt and freshly milled pepper

$\frac{1}{4}$ cup chopped fresh parsley

1 Heat the oil in a large stockpot over medium heat. Add the leek and cook until tender, about 3 minutes. Add the garlic and sauté for another minute. Add the sherry, stock, and cumin. Raise the heat, bring to a boil, add the mussels, and cover. Boil for about 6 minutes, until the shells open.

2 Season to taste with salt and pepper. Top with the parsley and serve.

ORIGINAL RECIPE

Mussels: Mix liquamen [fermented fish sauce], chopped leeks, cumin, sweet raisin wine, savory, and wine. Dilute the mixture with water and cook the mussels in it.

— *ON COOKERY*, APICIUS

⊡

THE OLYMPICS, named for the Greek town Olympia, began in 776 B.C. These sports events honoring the god Zeus were held every four years in either August or September and usually lasted five days. Originally the only competition was a 200-meter sprint, but by the fifth century B.C., other events such as long-jumping, javelin hurling, boxing, wrestling, discus throwing, and chariot races were added. Participants competed either completely nude or wearing only a thong.

Only males and unmarried women were allowed to watch the Olympics. Presumably unmarried women were permitted so that they could better evaluate prospective grooms' essential qualities.

FREE-FORM CHERRY LASAGNA

Serves 4

Closed lips hurt no one, speaking may.

—CATO THE ELDER, 234—149 B.C.

The original recipe describes sheets of dry, thin bread dough layered with cheese, perhaps an ancestor to the modern-day Greek cheese pie and Italian lasagna. When I prepared it exactly as described in the original, the results were a little dry, so I created a sauce based on a fruit compote recipe of the time.

This unusual free-form lasagna with tart cherry sauce is just sweet enough to spark the appetite but not so sweet as to be dessertlike. If you have difficulty finding tart cherries, fresh apricots are a delicious substitute. One of my wonderful recipe testers, Judy Borger, prepared this as a side dish for duck using cranberries, the decidedly all-American fruit, with outstanding results.

2 shallots, minced

1 tablespoon plus 2 teaspoons olive oil, plus more as needed

$\frac{1}{2}$ cup white wine

$\frac{1}{2}$ cup vegetable stock

$1\frac{1}{2}$ cups pitted fresh, canned, or frozen tart cherries

Grated zest of $\frac{1}{2}$ lemon

4 lasagna sheets

1 bay leaf

6 whole allspice berries

1 cup whole-milk ricotta cheese

2 tablespoons grated Parmesan cheese

Pinch of ground white pepper

Pinch of ground nutmeg

2 tablespoons sesame seeds, toasted

Shaved Parmesan cheese for garnish

1   Bring a large pot of salted water to a boil.

2   Sauté half of the shallots in 1 tablespoon of the oil in a saucepan over medium heat until softened, about 3 minutes. Add the wine, stock, and cherries, and bring to a boil. Cook until the cherries are very soft and the liquid has mostly evaporated, about 15 minutes. Allow to cool slightly, then pulse in a food processor until coarsely chopped. Return the mixture to the pan, stir in the zest, cover, and keep warm over very low heat.

3   Once the water is boiling, add the lasagna sheets, bay leaf, and allspice, and cook according to package directions. Drain in a colander, remove the bay leaf and allspice, and toss lightly with a few drops of oil to keep from sticking.

4   Stir together the ricotta and grated Parmesan cheeses, white pepper, and nutmeg in a small bowl until combined. Heat 2 teaspoons of the oil in a small saucepan over low heat. Add the remaining shallots and cook until softened, about 3 minutes. Add half of the cheese mixture to the shallots and stir until combined. Remove from the heat and stir in the remaining cheese mixture.

5   To assemble, cut a lasagna sheet in half. Spread about 1 teaspoon of cherry sauce on a serving plate. Lay the half sheet of lasagna on the sauce. On one end place 1 tablespoon of cheese, fold, and top with a little more cherry sauce. Repeat with the other half sheet of lasagna on the same plate. Repeat the entire procedure with the other 3 sheets of lasagna. Garnish each plate with the sesame seeds and shaved Parmesan. Serve immediately.

*You can list neither all the virtues of fine flour, nor all its uses,
how often it serves the baker and the cook.*

—MARTIAL, A.D. 40–103

THE ROMANS used flour and even the starchy water from cooking grains to thicken sauces. Still today many Italian chefs use this method to control the consistency of sauce.

ASSORTED FIG APPETIZERS
Serves 6

I call a fig, a fig; a spade, a spade.
—MENANDER, 342—292 B.C.

Plato was often referred to as a "fig lover" because of his extreme fondness for these succulent morsels. The ancients believed that figs, one of the oldest cultivated fruits, brought pleasant dreams and should be eaten before dinner, "when the appetite is virgin."

Here, three different tantalizing fillings for figs provide a perfect assortment of tastes to start any elegant meal.

18 whole dried figs

1 cup white wine

3 teaspoons mascarpone cheese

Grated zest of $\frac{1}{2}$ lemon

2 tablespoons finely chopped pistachio nuts

1 teaspoon honey

2 ounces thinly sliced prosciutto

1   Bring the figs and wine to a simmer in a saucepan over low heat until the figs are soft, about 5 minutes. Remove the figs with a slotted spoon. Continue cooking the wine until very thick and syrupy, about 10 minutes. Reserve.

2   Cut $\frac{1}{4}$ inch off the tops of 6 figs and set the figs, cut side up, on a serving platter. Top each with $\frac{1}{2}$ teaspoon of the cheese and sprinkle with the lemon zest.

3   Remove the stems from 6 more figs and halve the figs lengthwise. Pile the pistachios on a small plate and press the cut portion of each fig into them until the nuts adhere. Arrange the pistachio fig halves on the serving platter and drizzle with a little honey.

4   Remove the stems from the remaining figs and halve the figs crosswise. Make a small cavity in each center with the tip of your finger. Cut the prosciutto into $\frac{1}{2}$-inch-wide strips, roll into a bundle, and press into each fig. Place the stuffed figs on the serving platter and drizzle with the wine syrup.

THERE are numerous references in antiquity to Greek athletes eating figs to build stamina and muscle. Hercules, an athlete of heroic proportions, reportedly enjoyed fresh figs for dessert.

Hercules was renowned not only for his amazing strength but also for his rather limited intellect. According to legend, on one hot summer day he was seen shouting insults at the sun and threatening to shoot it with an arrow if the weather didn't cool down immediately. On another occasion, while on a choppy boat ride, Hercules screamed at the waves and warned that he'd beat them if they didn't calm down.

SMOKED TROUT CUSTARD WITH DILL

Serves 4

Everything that deceives may be said to enchant.

—PLATO, 428–348 B.C.

The Romans enjoyed amusing their guests by serving whimsical dishes. Often one ingredient was disguised as another; for example, liver pâté was set in a fish mold and called "salt fish without fish."

Regarding this smoked trout recipe, Apicius, a Roman chef, delightedly pointed out that guests would be astonished by fish served in a custard form. Sea nettles, or jellyfish, were added to the original dish to help solidify it. This modern version omits the jellyfish but keeps the other marvelous flavors. Rich and creamy, this custard is beautifully complemented with salty capers and tangy shallots.

3 large egg yolks

1 large egg

$1\frac{1}{4}$ cups half-and-half

2 teaspoons freshly squeezed lemon juice

2 teaspoons chopped fresh dill, plus fronds for garnish

$\frac{1}{2}$ teaspoon dry mustard

$\frac{1}{2}$ teaspoon salt

4 ounces smoked trout, finely flaked

2 tablespoons capers

2 tablespoons finely minced shallots

Toast points

1 Preheat the oven to 400° F.

2 Put four $\frac{1}{2}$-cup ramekins into a casserole dish and set aside.

3 Whisk together the yolks, egg, half-and-half, lemon juice, chopped dill, mustard, and salt in a large bowl until well combined.

4 Divide the trout among the ramekins. Pour the custard mixture evenly into each ramekin. Fill the casserole dish with hot water halfway up the sides of the ramekins.

5 Bake on the center rack of the oven until set, 25 to 30 minutes. Remove the ramekins from the water bath and allow to cool.

6 When the custards are cool, run a sharp knife around the edge of each and invert onto a serving plate. Serve with the capers and shallots and toast points. Garnish each custard with a dill frond.

ORIGINAL RECIPE

Patina of anchovy without anchovy. Take fillets of grilled or boiled fish and mince enough to fill a pan of the size you wish. Pound pepper and a little rue. Add sufficient liquamen [fermented fish sauce]. Break eggs and stir in. Add a little oil, and mix everything in the pan with the fish, so that it forms a smooth mixture. On top of this you place jellyfish, taking care that they do not mix with the eggs. Cook in the steam so that the jellyfish cannot combine with the eggs, and when they are dry sprinkle with ground pepper and serve. At table no one will know what he is eating!

—*ON COOKERY*, APICIUS

MEAT was a luxury in ancient times, so the main meal typically consisted of thick soups and stews of assorted grains, vegetables, and legumes.

Aesop tells a tit-for-tat soup fable about a mean-spirited wolf who spitefully invited a crane to dinner and served thin broth on a flat rock, which was impossible for the crane to drink because of its long beak. The crane retaliated by inviting the wolf to a meal of soup served in a narrow and long-necked container, poorly suited to the guest's thick muzzle.

Chapter 2

FIRE:
SOUPS AND STEWS

GOLDEN BEET SHERRY-CUMIN SOUP

VEGETABLE AND BEAN BARLEY SOUP

FENNEL PUREE

PORT OF NAPLES SEAFOOD STEW WITH
ALMOND PESTO CROSTINI

HERBED BARLEY WITH PANCETTA

VEAL AND FIG STEW

CHESTNUT-MINT PUREE

LEMONY CELERY AND LEEK PUREE

FRAGRANT LAMB AND COUSCOUS STEW

SPRING PEA AND FENNEL PUREE

ROMAN SWEET-AND-TART FISH CHOWDER

GOLDEN BEET SHERRY-CUMIN SOUP

Serves 4

There are two liquids especially agreeable to the human body,
wine inside and oil outside.

—PLINY THE ELDER, A.D. 23—79

Wine, thought essential for good digestion, was always served at feasts. The ancients even had a derogatory term for a meal served without it: *caninum prandium,* literally, dinner for a dog.

Sweet wine and fragrant cumin combine here with beets for a soup so rich in flavor that it is sure to please vegetarians and meat lovers alike.

1 large sweet onion, diced

2 tablespoons extra virgin olive oil

3 large leeks, white and tender green parts, thinly sliced

8 baby golden beets, thinly sliced

$\frac{1}{2}$ cup sweet sherry

3 cups vegetable stock

1 teaspoon ground cumin

Salt and freshly milled pepper

2 cups finely chopped beet greens or Swiss chard

1 Sauté the onion in the oil in a stockpot over medium heat until golden, 8 to 10 minutes. Add the leeks and beets and continue cooking for about 5 minutes.

2 Stir in the sherry and simmer until reduced by half. Add the stock, cumin, and salt and pepper to taste, and cook until the beets are tender, about 20 minutes. Remove from the heat and gently stir in the beet greens.

THE PHYSICIAN'S OATH, written by Hippocrates in the fifth century B.C., begins "I swear by Apollo Physician . . . in whatsoever houses I enter, I will enter to help the sick, and I will abstain from all intentional wrongdoing." The Hippocratic oath, in disuse for more than a thousand years, was reinstated in medical schools during the Renaissance and is still used today by graduating physicians.

Hippocrates' medical treatments were gentle and included baths, simple herbals, and prescribed modifications in diet and exercise. He sensibly taught that there was no one perfect health regimen for everyone and that illness and health were found equally in "those who drink wine as much as those who abstain, . . . those who take much exercise as those who take little."

VEGETABLE AND BEAN BARLEY SOUP

Serves 10

Tomatoes, a New World food introduced into Europe in the late fifteenth century, were totally unknown to the ancient Greeks and Romans. Other foods imported from the Americas after Columbus include bell peppers, potatoes, vanilla, and chocolate.

You'll never miss the tomatoes in this rich and flavorful bean soup. Thickened with split peas and barley, it is perfect for chilly autumn and winter evenings.

1 large onion, diced

$1/4$ cup olive oil

2 leeks, white and tender green parts, thinly sliced

1 fennel bulb, diced, plus fronds for garnish

2 celery ribs with leaves, diced

1 cup diced red cabbage

1 quart vegetable or chicken stock

$1/4$ cup barley

$3/4$ cup cooked chickpeas, rinsed and drained

$1/3$ cup green split peas

$1/3$ cup lentils

1 teaspoon dried marjoram

1 teaspoon dried fennel seeds

1 teaspoon ground coriander

Salt and freshly milled pepper

$1/4$ cup minced fresh dill

1 Sauté the onion in the oil in a large soup pot over medium heat until softened, about 10 minutes. Add the leeks, diced fennel, celery, and cabbage, and sauté for another 10 minutes.

2 Raise the heat to high. Add the stock and barley plus 3 cups of water. Bring to a low boil and simmer for 10 minutes. Add the chickpeas, split peas, lentils, marjoram, fennel seeds, coriander, and salt and pepper to taste.

3 Simmer over medium heat until the beans and grains are tender, about 30 minutes.

4 Remove from the heat. Stir in the fresh dill and garnish with fennel fronds.

ORIGINAL RECIPE

Barley Soup with Dried Vegetables. Soak chickpeas, lentils, and peas. Crush barley, and boil with the dried vegetables. When it has boiled long enough, add sufficient oil, and chop the following greens: leeks, coriander, dill, fennel, beet, mallow, and tender cabbage. Put all these finely chopped greens into the saucepan. Boil cabbage. Pound a generous quantity of fennel seed, marjoram, silphium [a now extinct plant from Africa similar to bitter-tasting asafetida], lovage, and after pounding blend with liquamen [fermented fish sauce]. Pour over the dried vegetables and stir. Put chopped cabbage leaves on top.

— ON COOKERY, APICIUS

NOT ALL dinners in antiquity were formal affairs. In fact, the ancient Greeks even had an expression, "salt and bean friends," referring to close friends who were content to dine together on simple foods.

FENNEL PUREE

Serves 6

So gladiators fierce and rude
Mingled it with their daily food.
And he who battled and subdued
A wreath of fennel wore.

—HENRY WADSWORTH LONGFELLOW, 1807—1882

As Longfellow noted in his nineteenth-century poem, fennel was considered an important part of a healthy diet for gladiators, and wreaths of it were given to victorious combatants. Depending on the occasion, plants such as bay laurel, long grass, rose, and myrtle were used to make ceremonial wreaths. Olive leaves were reserved for Olympian winners and oak leaves for someone who saved a man in battle.

As directed in the original Roman recipe, the splash of vinegar added at the end of cooking gives a nice fresh taste to this light fennel soup, which is also wonderful served cold.

1 large onion, sliced

2 tablespoons extra virgin olive oil

1 large fennel bulb, sliced

2 celery ribs with leaves, diced

1 quart vegetable or chicken stock

1 teaspoon ground coriander

Salt and freshly milled pepper

2 tablespoons minced fresh cilantro

$\frac{1}{4}$ cup minced fresh mint

2 tablespoons honey

3 tablespoons muscatel or sherry vinegar

2 tablespoons minced fennel fronds

1 Sauté the onion in the oil in a large soup pot over medium heat until softened, about 10 minutes. Add the sliced fennel and celery, and continue cooking until tender, 6 to 8 minutes.

2 Add the stock and coriander, and season to taste with salt and pepper. Simmer, covered, until all the vegetables are tender, about 20 minutes. Remove from the heat and add the cilantro, mint, honey, and vinegar. Puree in batches in a blender.

3 Serve the soup garnished with the minced fennel fronds.

SLAVES, prisoners, and captured enemy soldiers were often forced to become gladiators. Occasionally, free men, attracted by the potential for financial reward and fame, volunteered.

Gladiator spectacles were sponsored by a town or paid for by politicians wanting to garner support from the citizens. These events always drew large audiences from neighboring areas who were made aware of the games by notices posted by paid artists.

A school for gladiators, uncovered at Pompeii, included a cafeteria and dormitory as well as indoor and outdoor training areas. Discovered within the rubble were helmets, weapons, metal-mesh protective gear, shields, and equestrian equipment. In the ruins of one private home was a collection of the names, preferred weapons, and number of battles fought by more than twenty-five gladiators. Apparently collecting gladiator statistics was just as popular a hobby then as collecting baseball cards is today.

PORT OF NAPLES SEAFOOD STEW WITH ALMOND PESTO CROSTINI

Serves 6

In Rome you long for the country; in the country—oh inconstant!—you praise the distant city to the stars.

—HORACE, 65—8 B.C.

This recipe was originally named after the fashionable seaside resort town of Baiae, near the Bay of Naples. It was prized for its volcanic hot springs, and many wealthy Romans, including Nero, owned second homes there. It remained a popular spot until well into the third century when a series of earthquakes caused its decline.

This delicious stew, which is hearty enough to make a main course, is ready in less than thirty minutes. The almond pesto crostini add a delicious crunch, so be sure to make lots of them to absorb every drop of the mouthwatering broth.

1 large sweet onion, diced

3 celery ribs with leaves, diced

$\frac{1}{2}$ cup extra virgin olive oil

2 garlic cloves, minced

$\frac{1}{2}$ teaspoon ground cumin

$\frac{1}{2}$ teaspoon ground coriander

1 cup white wine

2 dozen littleneck clams, in shells, scrubbed

2 pounds mussels, in shells, scrubbed and debearded

8 ounces small shrimp, peeled and deveined

8 ounces sea scallops

$\frac{3}{4}$ cup minced fresh parsley

Salt and freshly milled pepper

2 tablespoons slivered almonds

4 large green Sicilian olives, pitted

2 tablespoons small capers, rinsed

12 baguette slices, toasted

1 Sauté the onion and celery in ¼ cup of the oil in a large stockpot over medium heat until the onion is translucent, about 8 minutes. Add the garlic, cumin, coriander, and wine. Raise the heat to high and bring to a boil. Boil for 2 to 3 minutes to reduce the wine.

2 Add the clams and mussels, and cook until the shells open, about 4 minutes. Add the shrimp and scallops, and continue cooking until the scallops are opaque and cooked through, 1 to 2 minutes. Remove from the heat, stir in ½ cup of the minced parsley, and season to taste with salt and pepper.

3 Puree the almonds, olives, capers, and remaining ¼ cup of parsley in a food processor until smooth. Slowly add the remaining ¼ cup of oil and continue to puree until well blended. Spread a bit of pesto on each toasted baguette slice and serve with the warm stew.

NERO, the first-century Roman emperor whose extravagances were legendary, once spent the equivalent of $100,000 on Egyptian roses for one banquet. According to Suetonius, the first-century biographer, Nero built a fantastic dining room, operated with gears and pulleys, that was "circular and constantly revolved, day and night, like the heavens."

HERBED BARLEY WITH PANCETTA

Serves 6

A wise man should consider health the greatest of human blessings.

—HIPPOCRATES, 460—377 B.C.

Barley's healthful properties were widely understood; in fact, Hippocrates prescribed a diet consisting solely of cereals and breads made from barley for the duration of an illness.

This thick barley stew, beautifully speckled with bright carrots and herbs, can be served as a grain side dish, a hearty main-course lunch, or a first-course starter.

4 ounces pancetta, diced

1 medium onion, diced

1 garlic clove, minced

1 carrot, halved and thinly sliced

1 celery rib with leaves, thinly sliced

1 leek, white and tender green parts, thinly sliced

1 bay leaf

$\frac{1}{2}$ teaspoon dried savory

$\frac{1}{4}$ cup chopped fresh dill

1 cup pearl barley

1 quart chicken stock

$\frac{1}{3}$ cup lentils

Salt and freshly milled pepper

1   Sauté the pancetta and onion in a large stockpot over medium heat until golden, about 10 minutes.

2   Add the garlic, carrot, celery, leek, bay leaf, and savory. Sauté until the vegetables become tender, about 5 minutes. Raise the heat, add 2 tablespoons of the dill, the barley, and the stock, and bring to a boil.

3   Lower the heat, cover, and slow-boil for 45 minutes. Add the lentils and continue cooking until tender, 15 to 20 minutes.

4. Remove the bay leaf and season to taste with salt and pepper. Serve topped with the remaining 2 tablespoons of fresh dill.

HIPPOCRATES analyzed a patient's dreams to help diagnose illness, noting, "He who has learnt aright about the signs that come in sleep will find that they have an important influence upon all things." According to Hippocrates, once we fall asleep, our mind is freed of external stimuli and can explore the messages given by the body regarding its internal condition. For Hippocrates, if someone is healthy in body and mind, he more or less dreams about things dealing with normal daily activities. However, dreams about extraordinary events indicate potential problems. If, for example, a patient dreams about torrential rains, it might be an indication of kidney problems. Dreams of "fruitless trees" were thought to reveal reproductive difficulties such as impotence or infertility.

Interestingly, Hippocrates observed that patients often have frightening nightmares of "monstrous bodies" after a too-heavy meal.

VEAL AND FIG STEW

Serves 4

The fool looks for figs in winter.

—MARCUS AURELIUS, A.D. 121—180

This ancient Roman recipe for veal slow-cooked with figs reminds me of the many meat and fruit stews found throughout Greece today. Meat cooked with figs becomes amazingly tender, and this fork-tender veal in savory sweet broth gets just the perfect crunch from almonds. This is a sure crowd-pleaser and one of my family's favorite dishes.

1 large sweet onion, thickly sliced

3 celery ribs with leaves, thickly sliced

3 tablespoons extra virgin olive oil

1 pound boneless veal, cut into 1-inch cubes

Salt and freshly milled pepper

All-purpose flour for dredging

$\frac{1}{4}$ cup fruit vinegar

2 teaspoons fennel seeds

1 tablespoon dried marjoram

3 cups beef stock

5 whole dried figs, diced

1 teaspoon prepared honey mustard

$\frac{1}{4}$ cup slivered almonds, toasted

$\frac{1}{4}$ cup minced fresh parsley

1   Sauté the onion and celery in 1 tablespoon of the oil in a heavy-bottomed stockpot over medium heat until golden, 8 to 10 minutes. Remove and set aside.

2   Season the veal with salt and pepper, and dredge in flour. Raise the heat to high, add the remaining 2 tablespoons of oil and the veal cubes, and brown on all sides. Pour in the vinegar and cook, stirring, until the vinegar has been absorbed by the meat.

3   Add the fennel seeds, marjoram, stock, and figs. Adjust the heat to low, cover, and simmer for 30 minutes.

4   Add the mustard and the reserved onion and celery. Continue cooking until the veal is tender, another 30 minutes. Season to taste with salt and pepper.

5   To serve, top with the almonds and parsley.

ORIGINAL RECIPE

Veal: pepper, lovage, fennel seed, marjoram, nuts, fig-dates, honey, vinegar, liquamen [fermented fish sauce], mustard, and oil.

—*ON COOKERY,* APICIUS

CHESTNUT-MINT PUREE

Serves 4

The original recipe wisely advises, "Taste. If something is missing, add it," reminding us that seasoning should always be adjusted after cooking.

This soup is quick to prepare using ready-roasted chestnuts sold in glass jars. As advised by the ancient Romans, just before serving, top with a drizzle of virgin olive oil to add extra richness and flavor. Makes a perfect lunch served with crusty bread and a green salad.

1 large sweet onion, diced

1 tablespoon extra virgin olive oil

1 quart vegetable or chicken stock

$\frac{1}{2}$ cup lentils

1 teaspoon ground cumin

1 teaspoon ground coriander

$1\frac{1}{2}$ cups roasted and peeled chestnuts

12 to 15 fresh mint leaves

Salt and freshly milled pepper

1   Sauté the onion in the oil in a large stockpot over medium heat until golden, about 10 minutes. Raise the heat to high and add the stock, lentils, cumin, and coriander. Bring to a boil. Add the chestnuts, reserving 1 to be finely minced for garnish.

2   Lower the heat to medium, cover, and cook until the lentils are tender, 15 to 20 minutes. Puree the soup and mint leaves in a blender or food processor. Season to taste with salt and pepper. Serve topped with the reserved minced chestnut.

THERE were many public libraries in antiquity, but unlike modern ones, most did not allow borrowing. Unearthed at an Athens library was a stone with the inscription "No book shall be taken out, for we have sworn."

The library of Alexandria, Egypt, housed more than five hundred thousand papyrus rolls in antiquity. Sadly, over the years, worms—called "the worst enemy of the muses"—as well as mold and fire destroyed most of the collection.

In addition to a few complete works, odd fragments have survived that include contracts between everyday citizens such as divorce agreements, contracts to hire a wet nurse, agreements to rent private dining rooms, and bakery leases. Also surviving are letters requesting the purchase of foods for feasts. One reads, "Send the fish on the 24th or 25th for Gemella's birthday feast," and another states, "Send me also as many cheeses as you can, empty jars, vegetables of all sorts, and any delicacies that you may have." A third request was for "a good pig for our party, but again, let it be a good one, and not lean and unfit to eat like the last."

Probably my favorite document is a list of household expenses by an unknown Roman that includes an entry for "carpenter's glue for the wheels of the racing chariot." Reading it suddenly brought the past vividly into the present, reminding me that the chariots seen in countless movies were once real and driven not only by gladiators but also by ordinary Roman citizens.

LEMONY CELERY AND LEEK PUREE

Serves 6

Reducing stock and adding eggs to thicken and season soup are two techniques from antiquity still valued today.

This modern version of a Roman recipe is an elegant but easy-to-prepare soup. In Roman times, delicious vegetarian soups like this one were often prescribed as essential for "promoting good health." Be sure to use some of the tender inner leaves from the celery; they add extra flavor to this wonderful puree that is also delightful served cold. Photograph on page 58.

3 tablespoons olive oil

4 leeks, white and tender green parts, diced

6 celery ribs with leaves, diced

1 quart vegetable or chicken stock

Salt and freshly milled pepper

1 large egg, lightly beaten

Juice and grated zest of 2 lemons

1 Heat the oil in a large saucepan over medium heat. Add the leeks and celery, and sauté until the celery is tender, about 10 minutes.

2 Add the stock and season to taste with salt and pepper. Bring to a boil, lower the heat, cover, and simmer for about 30 minutes.

3 Puree the soup in batches in a blender or food processor until smooth. Return the soup to the pot and warm over medium heat. Mix the egg and lemon juice together and slowly whisk into the soup. Serve garnished with the lemon zest.

ORIGINAL RECIPE

Another vegetable dish promoting good health. Wash celery, greens, and roots, and dry it in the sun; then also cook the tender part and head of leeks in a new pot, allowing the water to boil down one-third of its volume. Thereupon grind pepper with broth and honey in equal amounts properly measured, mix it in the mortar with the water of the cooked celery, strain, boil again, and serve at once, adding the celery if liked.

—*ON COOKERY*, APICIUS

FRAGRANT LAMB AND COUSCOUS STEW

Serves 6

Marinating the lamb in herbs and olive oil overnight imparts a wonderful fragrance and taste to this outstanding stew. Taking my cue from the ancients, I now keep a small jar of olive oil in the kitchen and add bits of assorted herbs left over from other recipes. The resulting oil is great for vinaigrettes, for sautéing vegetables, and for quick seasoning for grilled fish. Almost any mix of herbs adds a wonderful flavor to food.

You'll want to take the advice of the second-century B.C. Greek poet Nicander, who suggested using "bread spoons" to scoop up every flavorful bit of this delectable stew.

2 long sprigs fresh rosemary, plus more for garnish

1 bay leaf

$\frac{1}{2}$ teaspoon coriander seeds

6 whole allspice berries

$\frac{1}{4}$ cup extra virgin olive oil, plus more as needed

$2\frac{1}{2}$ pounds boneless leg of lamb, cut into $1\frac{1}{2}$-inch cubes

Salt and freshly milled pepper

All-purpose flour for dredging

2 large sweet onions, quartered

3 celery ribs, thickly sliced

3 garlic cloves, minced

$1\frac{1}{2}$ cups white wine

1 quart plus 3 cups chicken stock

$\frac{1}{2}$ teaspoon cumin seeds

1 large red onion

2 cups Israeli couscous

$\frac{1}{4}$ cup minced fresh parsley

1   Mix the rosemary, bay leaf, coriander, allspice, and oil in a large bowl. Add the lamb cubes, toss well, cover with plastic wrap, and refrigerate. Allow the flavors to mingle for at least 1 hour or overnight.

2   Position 2 racks in the oven and preheat to 350° F.

3   Remove the lamb from the marinade, generously season it with salt and pepper, and dredge in flour. Strain the oil to remove the herbs and seeds, reserving them. Put the strained oil in a heavy ovenproof Dutch oven. Heat the scented oil over high heat and cook the lamb in batches until golden on all sides. Set the browned meat aside.

4   Add the sweet onions and celery to the pot, and add another tablespoon of oil if needed. Keeping the heat on high, brown the onions for 3 to 4 minutes. Lower the heat to medium, add the garlic, and cook for another minute. Return the meat to the pot, add the wine, and simmer until the wine is reduced by half, about 4 minutes.

5   Stir to release the bits of cooked meat at the bottom of the pot, then add 1 quart of the stock, the cumin seeds, and the reserved herbs. Bring to a boil, cover the pot, and remove from the heat. Transfer to the lower rack of the oven and bake for 45 minutes.

6   Meanwhile, cut the red onion into ¼-inch wedges, toss with oil, season with salt and pepper, and place on a nonstick baking sheet. When the lamb has baked for 25 minutes, put the onion wedges on the upper rack to roast for the final 20 minutes of cooking time.

7   Bring the remaining 3 cups of stock to a boil in a saucepan over medium heat. Stir in the couscous and simmer for 10 minutes, or until the liquid has been absorbed. When the lamb and onion wedges are cooked, remove from the oven. Take out and discard the bay leaf and stir in the cooked couscous until it is well coated with the sauce. Cover the pot and allow to stand for 5 minutes before serving.

8   Ladle the stew into serving bowls and top with the roasted red onion, rosemary sprigs, and the parsley.

BOOKS were sold in ancient Greece as early as the fifth century B.C. At that time books were handwritten on rolled papyrus scrolls. It was the Romans who later developed the square and rectangular book shapes we know today.

Spring Pea and Fennel Puree
and Lemony Celery and Leek Puree

SPRING PEA
AND FENNEL PUREE
Serves 6

I found Rome a city of bricks and left it a city of marble.

—AUGUSTUS CAESAR, 63 B.C.—A.D. 14

This delicious pea soup was originally named for Vitellius, an emperor of Rome during A.D. 69, the period referred to as "the year of four emperors." Vitellius, a legendary gourmet, was reported to have bankrupted whole towns; they were "ruined by having to provide for his feasts." Although initially honored for his military exploits, he was ultimately ousted from power. As an angry crowd of Roman citizens jeered, Vitellius philosophically reflected, "And yet I was once your emperor."

This soup, although best made with young spring peas, is also spectacular using frozen peas. If you like, you can garnish it with lovely edible spring flowers, as was done in ancient Rome. But no matter how you garnish it, this combination of peas and fennel, which is also delicious cold, makes an imperial first course.

1 large leek, white and tender green parts, sliced

3 tablespoons olive oil

$\frac{1}{2}$ cup plus 2 tablespoons white wine

1 quart vegetable or chicken stock

1 fennel bulb, thinly sliced, plus fronds for garnish

12 ounces peas

1 teaspoon ground coriander

1 teaspoon dried marjoram

Salt and freshly milled pepper

Wild edible flowers (optional)

1 Sauté the leek in the oil in a large soup pot over medium heat until tender, about 3 minutes. Raise the heat to high, add $\frac{1}{2}$ cup of the wine, and boil until reduced by half, 3 to 4 minutes. Add the stock, fennel, peas, coriander, and marjoram, and bring to a boil. Lower the heat to medium and cook for about 12 minutes, until the peas are tender.

2 Puree in batches in a blender or food processor until smooth. Season to taste with salt and pepper, and add the remaining 2 tablespoons of wine. Garnish with the fennel fronds and the wild edible flowers, if using, and serve.

ROMAN SWEET-AND-TART FISH CHOWDER

Serves 6

But what can be considered of greater authority than the senses?

—LUCRETIUS, 100—55 B.C.

This chowder was originally named after Lucretius, the first-century B.C. poet who wrote much of what we know about Epicureanism. This philosophy, developed by Epicurus, was based on the premise that to achieve happiness man should strive to avoid pain and seek pleasure. Interestingly, the Epicureans frowned on gluttony and hedonism because they knew that excess ultimately brought pain.

The delightful combination of sweet onions and tart vinegar served with fish is still popular in the Mediterranean region today. This is truly a soup worthy of its Epicurean namesake.

3 large sweet onions, diced

2 tablespoons olive oil

$\frac{1}{2}$ cup white wine vinegar

2 tablespoons honey

1 quart fish or vegetable stock

1 teaspoon dried oregano

8 ounces cod, cut into $\frac{1}{2}$-inch chunks

Salt and freshly milled pepper

Fresh oregano leaves (optional)

1   Sauté the onions in the oil in a large soup pot over low heat for 20 minutes, until very soft. Raise the heat to high and cook the onions until golden, about 5 minutes.

2   Add the vinegar and honey. Stirring frequently, boil until the vinegar reduces to just a few tablespoons, 3 to 4 minutes.

3   Add the stock and dried oregano, and bring to a boil. Lower the heat and simmer for about 10 minutes.

4   Puree the soup in a blender or food processor.

5   Return the soup to the soup pot, add the cod, and cook for 12 to 15 minutes, until the fish is cooked through. Season to taste with salt and pepper.

6   Serve topped with fresh oregano, if using.

ORIGINAL RECIPE

Lucretian Dish. Clean spring onions, throw away their green, and chop into a shallow pan. Add a little liquamen [fermented fish sauce], oil, and water. While it cooks put raw salt fish in the center. But as soon as it is all nearly cooked add a teaspoonful of honey and very little vinegar and reduced wine. Taste. If it is too sweet, add liquamen, if too salty a little honey. Sprinkle also with oregano and let it bubble.

— *ON COOKERY*, APICIUS

THE GREEKS created a lovely fable to account for nature's

wintertime dormancy.

According to myth, Hades, god of the underworld,

abducted Demeter's daughter, Persephone, to make

her his wife. Demeter, the goddess of harvest, was so

distraught at the loss of her child that she neglected her

duties, and all plants on earth soon withered and died.

Zeus intervened and ruled that Persephone had to

remain with Hades only one season each year.

This is why, according to legend, every winter when

Persephone is forced back to the underworld, Demeter

mourns and plants wither. When Persephone returns to

earth in spring, plants are reborn.

Chapter 3

EARTH:
SALADS AND
VEGETABLES

CUCUMBER WITH RAISIN-CORIANDER VINAIGRETTE

BABY GREENS WITH CAPER VINAIGRETTE

ARUGULA AND RADICCHIO WITH GINGER-DATE VINAIGRETTE

FIELD AND FOREST SALAD

FENNEL SALAD WITH MINT VINAIGRETTE

KALE WITH CORIANDER SAUCE

OVEN-ROASTED STRING BEANS

ACORN SQUASH WITH PINE NUTS AND HONEY

BRUSSELS SPROUTS WITH OLIVES, RAISINS, AND PINE NUTS

GRILLED CELERY WITH ANCHOVY-LEMON SAUCE

ROASTED LEEKS AND APPLE

PEA SOUFFLÉ WITH FRESH DILL

POPPY TURNIPS FOR KING NICOMEDES

BEETS WITH HONEY-WINE SYRUP

GOLDEN CHICKPEA CIRCLES

CUCUMBER WITH RAISIN-CORIANDER VINAIGRETTE

Serves 4

I have hardly ever known a mathematician
that was capable of reasoning.

—PLATO, 428—348 B.C.

Pythagoras, the sixth-century B.C. philosopher and mathematician who gave us the Pythagorean theorem, studied in Egypt. It was there he learned of a recipe for cucumbers, raisins, coriander, and mallow to relieve thirst that the goddess Demeter supposedly gave to Hercules. Mallow, a marsh herb, was thought to be a miracle food that prevented not only thirst but hunger as well.

In this modern version, feta, raisins, and spices are pureed to create a creamy, deliciously unusual dressing for cucumbers. This salad is excellent served with crusty dark bread and olives or as a cooling side dish for spicy foods.

1 European cucumber

2 ounces feta cheese

$1/4$ cup heavy cream

2 tablespoons fresh cilantro leaves, plus more for garnish

2 tablespoons muscatel or sherry vinegar

1 teaspoon honey

Juice of $1/2$ lemon

2 tablespoons extra virgin olive oil

$1/4$ teaspoon ground coriander

Salt and freshly milled pepper

3 tablespoons golden raisins

1　Cut the cucumber in half lengthwise and, using a knife or grapefruit spoon, remove the seeds. Coarsely grate the cucumber and reserve in a serving bowl.

2　Puree the cheese, cream, cilantro, vinegar, honey, lemon juice, oil, and coriander in a food processor until smooth. Add salt and pepper to taste and toss the vinaigrette with the cucumber. Top with the raisins and garnish with cilantro.

PYTHAGORAS, a vegetarian, stressed the importance of a nonmeat diet as the way to maintain physical and mental health and attain longevity. By many accounts he lived to be well over one hundred years old.

Pythagoras did not eat beans, either. Some scholars speculate that this was because of their association with bureaucracy, which he dreaded. In those days votes were cast with beans, and bureaucrats counted the bean ballots to determine the outcome of the vote. This practice is the origin of our present-day expression "bean counter."

BABY GREENS WITH
CAPER VINAIGRETTE
Serves 4

Galen, physician to Emperor Marcus Aurelius, wrote extensively on healthful eating and inspired this lovely tangy caper dressing. Galen recommended salads dressed with oil, honey, and vinegar for good digestion, and he advised eating capers for "whetting a jaded appetite."

There are many modern health authorities and chefs who advocate a raw-foods-only diet, a notion that has its roots in antiquity. Galen recounts a story of a medical student who "resolved never to light a fire." Eating only raw foods, the student "stayed healthy during all these years."

2 tablespoons freshly squeezed lemon juice

2 tablespoons wine vinegar

$3/4$ cup extra virgin olive oil

3 tablespoons capers, plus more for garnish

Salt and freshly milled pepper

3 cups assorted baby greens, such as arugula and spinach

1   Puree the lemon juice, vinegar, oil, and capers in a food processor until well blended. Season to taste with salt and pepper.

2   Toss the baby greens with the vinaigrette, place on a serving platter, and garnish with capers.

ARUGULA AND RADICCHIO WITH GINGER-DATE VINAIGRETTE

Serves 4

Lettuce once closed the dinners of our ancestors;
Tell me, why today does it open ours?

—MARTIAL, A.D. 40—103

According to this poem by Martial, the ancient Greeks ate salad at the end of the meal, a practice still in evidence today throughout Europe. This combination of semi-tart greens and sweet dressing is irresistible whether you enjoy it at the start or end of your meal.

3 tablespoons red wine vinegar

3 dates, sliced

$\frac{1}{2}$ teaspoon cumin seeds

1 tablespoon grated fresh ginger

1 tablespoon honey

$\frac{1}{4}$ cup olive oil

Salt and freshly milled pepper

1 small red onion, sliced into rounds

2 cups arugula

1 cup shredded radicchio, plus 4 whole leaves

1 cup finely grated Parmesan cheese

1. Combine the vinegar, dates, cumin seeds, ginger, and honey in a food processor and puree until well combined. Slowly pulse in the oil until blended. Season to taste with salt and pepper.

2. Mix the onion with 2 tablespoons of the vinaigrette and let stand for 5 minutes to reduce its sharpness. Toss the arugula and radicchio with the remaining vinaigrette and top with the onion.

3. To make a cheese "bowl," heat a nonstick skillet over medium-low heat. Sprinkle $\frac{1}{4}$ cup of the cheese in a thin, even layer in a circle about 8 inches in diameter in the center of the skillet. Cook until light golden brown, about 4 minutes. With a spatula, carefully slide

the round out of the pan and onto an inverted teacup or roll to form a bowl shape. Allow to cool completely before removing. Repeat the process to make 3 more bowls.

4   To serve, place each cheese bowl on a plate, line with a leaf of radicchio, and fill with the salad.

ORIGINAL RECIPE

Dress lettuces with oxyporum [a mixture of spices and dates], vinegar, and a little liquamen [fermented fish sauce] to make them more easily digestible, to prevent flatulence, and so that the lettuces cannot harm your system: 2 ounces cumin, 1 ounce ginger, 1 ounce fresh, $\frac{1}{2}$ ounce juicy dates, 1 ounce pepper, 9 ounces honey; the cumin may be Ethiopian, Syrian, or Libyan. When it has become dry bind everything with honey. When needed mix half a teaspoonful with vinegar and a little liquamen, or take half a teaspoonful after the meal.

—ON COOKERY, APICIUS

FIELD AND FOREST SALAD

Serves 4

Mushrooms have a wonderful woodsy fresh flavor and are delicious raw. Try this salad as a side dish with grilled foods or as a light starter, and be sure to experiment with various mushroom varieties such as chanterelles, oyster mushrooms, and morels.

$\frac{1}{4}$ cup extra virgin olive oil

3 tablespoons raspberry vinegar

Salt and freshly milled pepper

2 cups very thinly sliced assorted mushrooms

$\frac{3}{4}$ cup assorted fresh herbs, such as basil, mint, and parsley

2 tablespoons finely chopped pistachio nuts

In a small bowl, whisk together the oil and vinegar, and season to taste with salt and pepper. Arrange the mushrooms and herbs on a serving platter and drizzle on the vinaigrette. Top with the pistachios and serve immediately.

ORIGINAL RECIPE

Field and forest herbs can be eaten as they are, dipped in a dressing of liquamen [fermented fish sauce], oil, and vinegar, or cooked in a shallow pan with pepper, cumin, and mastic berries [related to pistachio nuts].

— *ON COOKERY*, APICIUS

POPULAR opinion about lettuce varied in ancient Greece; some raved about its healthful qualities, while others believed it caused everything from an upset stomach to impotence. The Pythagoreans believed lettuce would "relax desire" and even nicknamed it "eunuch." One Greek myth associates lettuce with a handsome lover's demise. Adonis, to escape the wrath of Aphrodite's other lover, hid in a lettuce bed, only to die anyway when his rival turned into a wild boar and killed him.

FENNEL SALAD WITH MINT VINAIGRETTE

Serves 6

This ancient Roman recipe is the forefather of the contemporary Sicilian classic, orange and fennel salad.

According to Greek myth, when Prometheus stole fire from Zeus, he hid it inside a stalk of fennel. In antiquity, fennel grew wild throughout the Mediterranean region and had many functions. Long stalks were fashioned into splints for sprains, teachers' pointers, and even wands for religious rituals.

This refreshing salad is a wonderful between-course palate cleanser or a side dish served with fish.

$\frac{1}{4}$ cup fresh mint leaves, plus more for garnish

3 tablespoons muscatel or sherry vinegar

1 tablespoon honey

$\frac{1}{4}$ cup extra virgin olive oil

Salt and freshly milled pepper

1 small red onion, thinly sliced

1 fennel bulb, thinly sliced

1 large citron or 2 lemons, peeled and thinly sliced

1 Grind the mint, vinegar, and honey in a food processor until finely minced. Slowly add the oil and pulse until well combined. Season to taste with salt and pepper.

2 Toss the vinaigrette with the onion and allow to rest for 5 to 10 minutes to soften the flavor. Add the fennel and citron, garnish with mint leaves, and serve.

ACCORDING to legend, in 490 B.C. a soldier ran 24.8 miles from the town of Marathon to Athens to announce Greece's victory over Carthage. To commemorate the battle, the Greeks ate olives with fennel, a plant that grew abundantly in Marathon.

The marathon, a 24.8-mile race, was part of the first modern Olympics that were held in Athens in 1896. In 1908, when the Olympics were hosted by England, the length of the marathon was changed from the original 24.8 miles to 26.2 miles, the distance from Windsor Castle to the stadium in London. After many years of heated debate, in 1924 the marathon distance was standardized to 26.2 miles.

KALE WITH CORIANDER SAUCE

Serves 6

Cato the Elder, the second-century B.C. Roman statesman, devoted several pages in his book *On Agriculture* to the "so-called Seven Good Things" about cabbage. According to him, cabbage can treat wounds, reduce swelling, set dislocated bones, and even prevent drunkenness. The ancients believed the cabbage was sacred, "the prophet among vegetables." A common exclamation at the time was "So help me cabbage!"

Kale, a dark green member of the cabbage family, is perfect for buffet suppers because it keeps its gorgeous color for a long while. The honey, coriander, and sweet vinegar seasoning is sure to please you and your guests, so help me cabbage!

3 large shallots, minced

2 tablespoons extra virgin olive oil

$\frac{1}{2}$ cup muscatel or sherry vinegar

2 tablespoons honey

1 teaspoon ground coriander

1 pound kale, chopped

Salt and freshly milled pepper

Sauté the shallots in the oil in a large skillet over medium heat until translucent, 3 to 4 minutes. Add the vinegar, honey, and coriander, and bring to a boil. Add the kale and sauté until tender, about 2 minutes. Season to taste with salt and pepper.

ORIGINAL RECIPE

If you eat it [cabbage] chopped, washed, dried, and seasoned with salt and vinegar, nothing will be more wholesome. That you may eat it with better appetite, sprinkle it with grape vinegar, and you will like it a little better when washed, dried, and seasoned with rue, chopped coriander, and salt.

—*ON AGRICULTURE,* CATO THE ELDER

OVEN-ROASTED STRING BEANS

Serves 6

Readers and listeners like my books,
Yet a certain poet calls them crude.
What do I care? I serve up food
To please my guests, not fellow cooks.

—MARTIAL, A.D. 40−103

Martial, who lived during the reign of Nero, wrote hundreds of short humorous poems or epigrams, which provide one of my favorite glimpses into the past. Martial unabashedly admits to sending honey cakes to elderly men in the hopes of a mention in their will and of finagling invitations to choice dinner parties. His poems touch on many aspects of daily life including men's talk at the public baths, Roman women's supposed promiscuity, gladiators sold at auction, snail forks, prostitution, and the virtues of bringing your own napkin to a dinner party.

This recipe for crisp roasted string beans is inspired by Martial's epigram describing a dinner he is planning.

1 pound string beans

1 medium red onion, thinly sliced into rounds

6 thin slices pancetta

1 tablespoon muscatel or sherry vinegar

Salt and freshly milled pepper

1   Preheat the oven to 450° F.
2   Arrange the string beans in one layer on the bottom of a baking pan. Top with the onion rounds and pancetta. Bake until the pancetta is crisp and the string beans are tender, 25 to 30 minutes.
3   Drizzle with the vinegar and season to taste with salt and pepper.

MARTIAL'S books of epigrams were often given to dinner guests as a parting gift.

Here are two of Martial's deliciously witty poems:

Although you're glad to be asked out, whenever you go,
you bitch and shout and bluster. You must stop being
rude: You can't enjoy free speech and food.

Three hundred guests, not one of whom I know—
And you, as host, wonder that I won't go.
Don't quarrel with me, I'm not being rude:
I can't enjoy sociable solitude.

Clockwise from top: Beets with Honey-Wine Syrup, Poppy Turnips for King Nicomedes, and Oven-Roasted String Beans

ACORN SQUASH WITH PINE NUTS AND HONEY

Serves 4

The Romans, acknowledging the culinary influences of Egypt, named this sumptuous dish after the city of Alexandria. Egypt's Queen Cleopatra maintained extremely close relations with the Romans and even gave birth to children fathered by Julius Caesar *and* Marc Antony. The splendor of Cleopatra's feasts was legendary. Cleopatra, who prided herself on originality, changed the furnishings and art in the dining room after each important meal, often giving away these treasures to departing dinner guests.

Warm squash slices topped with a hint of garlic and aromatic coriander is a dish fit for royalty.

1 acorn squash, about 1 pound

3 tablespoons extra virgin olive oil

2 garlic cloves, minced

$\frac{1}{4}$ cup minced fresh mint

Coarse sea salt and freshly milled pepper

$\frac{1}{4}$ cup muscatel or sherry vinegar

$\frac{1}{2}$ teaspoon ground cumin

$\frac{1}{2}$ teaspoon ground coriander

2 tablespoons honey

2 tablespoons pine nuts, toasted and coarsely ground

1 Seed the squash and cut it into $\frac{1}{4}$-inch-thick slices. Sauté the slices in the oil in a large non-stick skillet over medium heat until golden brown on both sides. Remove the squash from the pan and place on a serving platter. While still hot, top with the garlic, mint, and salt and pepper to taste.

2 In the same pan, bring the vinegar, cumin, coriander, and honey to a boil. Pour over the squash and top with the pine nuts. Serve warm or cold.

EGYPT'S fertile soil was well known to the ancient Greeks. When speaking of a leader with both admirable and negative qualities, the Greeks would often compare him to the produce of Egypt that yielded "both wholesome herbs, and drugs of deadly juice."

We know from several sources, including references in the Old Testament, that an Egyptian slave's diet included fish, cucumbers, cabbage, melons, onions, garlic, and leeks. Tomb excavations reveal a variety of foods enjoyed by the upper classes, such as sweetbreads, quail, pigeon, figs, berries, cheese, wine, and beer, as well as many types of breads and sweet cakes.

BRUSSELS SPROUTS WITH OLIVES, RAISINS, AND PINE NUTS

Serves 4

Apicius lists numerous recipes for brussels sprouts, so I prepared several as part of a taste-testing party. Hungry friends arrived, forks furiously flew, and ingredients collided. By unanimous opinion the combination of three recipes was the best recipe of all.

The resulting mix of salty tart olives, sweet raisins, and crunchy pine nuts combine with the brussels sprouts to make an unusual and delicious side dish that is sure to win over your own taste testers.

1 leek, white and tender green parts, thinly sliced

1 pint brussels sprouts, cut in half

2 tablespoons olive oil

$\frac{1}{4}$ cup vegetable or chicken stock

$\frac{1}{2}$ cup sliced green olives

$\frac{1}{4}$ cup golden raisins

Salt and freshly milled pepper

2 tablespoons pine nuts, toasted

1 Sauté the leek and brussels sprouts in the oil in a saucepan over high heat until the leek is golden, about 4 minutes. Add the stock, olives, and raisins, and adjust the heat to low. Simmer, covered, for 8 to 10 minutes, or until the sprouts are tender and the stock has been absorbed.

2 Season to taste with salt and pepper. Serve topped with the pine nuts.

GRILLED CELERY WITH ANCHOVY-LEMON SAUCE

Serves 4

Celebratory wreaths of celery leaves were given to winners of sporting events in the ancient world. Celery was also regarded as a symbol of mourning, and the Greek expression "A sprig of celery is all you can give him now" referred to someone fatally ill.

Although we usually eat celery raw, it is a nice change to serve it cooked, especially grilled. This superb sauce, similar to the modern Italian vegetable dip *bagna calda,* is irresistible.

12 celery ribs

Olive oil

1 garlic clove, minced

Juice of $\frac{1}{2}$ lemon

$\frac{1}{2}$ teaspoon dried marjoram

Salt and freshly milled pepper

5 oil-packed anchovy fillets

2 tablespoons chopped fresh parsley

Grated zest of 1 lemon

1   Prepare a charcoal fire in an outdoor grill or heat a countertop electric grill to medium. Brush the celery lightly with oil and grill until tender, about 2 minutes per side. Reserve.

2   Heat 3 tablespoons of oil in a small saucepan over medium heat. Add the garlic and cook until softened, 2 to 3 minutes. Stir in the lemon juice and marjoram, and season to taste with salt and pepper. Bring to a simmer and add the anchovies. Cook until the anchovies dissolve, about 1 minute. Remove from the heat and stir in the parsley.

3   To serve, pour the warm sauce over the grilled celery and garnish with the lemon zest.

ROASTED LEEKS AND APPLE

Serves 4

Virgil, among others, viewed farming as a noble undertaking. He wrote of a farmer who, although poor and owning only a tiny plot of land, was content: "In happiness he equaled the wealth of kings, and returning home late at night he used to load his table with banquets from his own land. First he was in the spring to gather roses, and apples in the fall; and when grim winter was still bursting rocks with her frost and braking the current of rivers with ice, already he was cutting soft-haired hyacinths."

This exceptionally delicious mix of leeks and apple makes a gorgeous side dish that is perfect with plain roasted meats or chicken. Simple to make, it's great for parties because you can easily double or triple the recipe.

2 tablespoons olive oil

2 tablespoons white wine

1 tablespoon honey

1 teaspoon dried marjoram

1 teaspoon anise seeds

3 large leeks, white and tender green parts

1 crisp apple, such as Granny Smith or Fiji, cored and sliced

Salt and freshly milled pepper

1   Preheat the oven to 400° F.

2   Whisk together the oil, wine, honey, marjoram, and anise seeds in a medium baking pan until combined. Quarter the leeks and slice into 2-inch pieces. Add the leeks and apple to the dressing, season to taste with salt and pepper, and toss to coat.

3   Bake for 30 minutes, stirring gently about every 10 minutes, until the leeks are golden and the apple is soft. Serve immediately.

PEA SOUFFLÉ WITH FRESH DILL
Serves 8

The qualities I admired in my father were his willingness to listen to any project for the common good; the unvarying insistence that rewards must depend on merit . . . and he was quite uncritical of the food he ate.

—MARCUS AURELIUS, A.D. 121—180

This recipe was originally named after Commodus, son of the emperor Marcus Aurelius. Commodus, who ruled after his father's death, routinely endangered his life by performing as a gladiator—a highly risky and undignified action considering his rank.

A vegetable soufflé makes a very dignified and only slightly risky side dish. The trick to soufflé is that it must be served immediately. However, for a risk-free variation, omit the eggs and serve the warm pea-dill puree alone as a side dish.

1 medium red onion, chopped

2 tablespoons olive oil

$\frac{1}{3}$ cup white wine

10 ounces peas, cooked and drained

$\frac{1}{3}$ cup fresh dill, plus more for garnish

Salt and freshly milled pepper

1 large egg yolk

3 large egg whites

1 Sauté the onion in the oil in a skillet over medium heat until golden, about 10 minutes. Add the wine, raise the heat to high, and boil until the wine is absorbed, about 3 minutes. Allow the mixture to cool.

2 Puree the cooked peas and the dill in a food processor or blender. Season to taste with salt and pepper. Add the onion mixture and egg yolk to the peas and puree. This mixture can remain in the refrigerator for up to 24 hours, until you are ready to make the soufflé.

3 Preheat the oven to 400° F.

4 Butter 8 individual ½-cup ramekins. In the bowl of an electric mixer, beat the egg whites with a pinch of salt until they form firm peaks.

5   Fold a quarter of the egg whites into the pea mixture to lighten it, and then fold in the remaining whites until just incorporated. Fill each ramekin three-quarters full with the pea mixture and place in a large, deep baking pan. Pour hot water into the pan until it reaches halfway up the sides of the ramekins. Bake on the center oven rack for 25 to 30 minutes, until lightly browned and set. Do not open the oven door during the first 25 minutes, or the soufflé may fall.

6   Garnish with dill, and serve immediately.

Your time has a limit set on it.

— MARCUS AURELIUS, A.D. 121–180

MARCUS AURELIUS, emperor of Rome, was a follower of Stoicism. This philosophy of self-discipline, founded in the third century B.C. in Greece, advocated a "striving after wisdom" and taught that happiness was not dependent on external factors. Aurelius believed in actively doing good, stressing that "a man does not sin by commission only, but often by omission."

Marcus Aurelius kept a personal journal that he entitled "To Himself"; it is better known to us today as *Meditations*. He did, in fact, meditate in "a space of quiet" when "distracted by outward cares."

POPPY TURNIPS
FOR KING NICOMEDES

Serves 4

This superb turnip recipe is inspired by the legend of a Greek king who, while traveling miles inland, craved a dish of anchovies. Wanting to please the king but not having anchovies, his chef sliced turnips into anchovy shapes. The chef seasoned, cooked, and topped them with "exactly forty seeds of black poppy," satisfying the king's craving.

These scrumptious turnips, which, of course, taste nothing like anchovies, make a delicious side vegetable for meat or poultry. Served with Beets with Honey-Wine Syrup (page 88), they create a luscious vegetarian appetizer. Even guests who think they don't like turnips will enjoy these camouflaged morsels. Photograph on page 77.

> 3 shallots, thinly sliced
>
> 2 tablespoons extra virgin olive oil
>
> 2 white turnips, julienned
>
> 3 tablespoons raspberry or fruit vinegar
>
> 3 tablespoons honey
>
> Salt and freshly milled pepper
>
> 2 tablespoons poppy seeds

1   Sauté the shallots in the oil in a nonstick skillet over medium heat until translucent, about 3 minutes. Add the turnips, vinegar, and honey, and season with salt and pepper to taste. Continue cooking, covered, for 15 to 20 minutes, or until the turnips are tender.

2   Sprinkle with the poppy seeds and serve.

VEGETARIANISM is an ancient practice. Pythagoras, the sixth-century B.C. mathematician and philosopher, ate no meat. His choice was based on reverence for animals and a belief in an afterlife for all creatures. Plutarch, the first-century Greek historian and philosopher, was also a vegetarian. For Plutarch, following a meatless diet was a matter of health, not ethics, since he believed meat "clouds the mind and dulls the intellect." He further contended, "It would be best to accustom oneself to no meat at all, for the earth affords plenty enough of things fit not only for nourishment but for delight and enjoyment."

BEETS WITH HONEY-WINE SYRUP

Serves 4

*The longest part of the journey is said to be
the passing of the front gate.*

—MARCUS VARRO, 116—27 B.C.

This dish was originally named after Marcus Varro, the first-century B.C. scholar and author commissioned by Julius Caesar to supervise the development of a Roman national library.

In his book *On Agriculture*, Varro explained various ways to farm for profit, including advice on raising snails, bees, and dormice. Since flowers were always in demand for Roman dinner parties, he also suggested growing and selling violets and roses.

Although Varro clearly loved agriculture, he readily acknowledged that farming was not for everyone. As he amusingly noted, there are those who "would rather hear about my feet than how beet-roots ought to be planted." Photograph on page 77.

4 medium red or golden beets, peeled and quartered

1 tablespoon olive oil

$^3/_4$ cup red or white wine

2 tablespoons honey

Coarse sea salt and freshly milled pepper

1 Toss the beets with the oil in a small saucepan. Pour the wine and honey over the beets and season to taste with salt and pepper.

2 Simmer, covered, until the beets are tender, about 20 minutes. Using a slotted spoon, remove the beets and continue cooking the wine mixture over medium heat until it is reduced to about 3 tablespoons.

3 Serve the beets topped with the honey-wine syrup.

ORIGINAL RECIPE

Beets Varro. Varro wrote: "Take beets, rub clean, and cook in honey-wine with a little salt and oil."

—*ON COOKERY,* APICIUS

GOLDEN CHICKPEA CIRCLES

Makes 15 fritters

It was well worth a trip to the health food store to track down chickpea flour for this recipe by Galen, a second-century physician. Amazingly versatile and high in protein, it creates many elegant yet economical dishes like these circles and Crisp Chickpea Wedges (page 174).

Using a frozen juice container you can not only store the chickpea batter but also make perfectly round circles that can be served just as you would polenta. Try them topped with melted cheese, sautéed mushrooms, or honey and coarse sea salt. This is a wonderful vegetarian snack, side dish, or appetizer.

$1\frac{1}{2}$ cups vegetable stock

$\frac{1}{2}$ teaspoon salt

$\frac{1}{4}$ teaspoon freshly milled pepper

1 cup chickpea flour

3 tablespoons olive oil

1 tablespoon honey

Coarse sea salt

1   Bring the stock, salt, and pepper to a boil in a medium saucepan. Adjust the heat to low and slowly whisk in the chickpea flour, breaking up any lumps that form. Simmer, stirring frequently, until thick, about 5 minutes. Remove from the heat and allow to cool slightly.

2   Pack the mixture into a clean, well-oiled 12-ounce frozen juice container and refrigerate for up to 3 days before using.

3   To remove, gently press on the sides of the juice container until the chickpea mixture slides out. Cut into $\frac{1}{4}$-inch slices.

4   Heat the oil in a large nonstick skillet over medium-high heat. Add the chickpea slices and fry, turning once, until golden, about 2 minutes per side.

5   Serve warm, topped with the honey and sea salt.

PLUTARCH, the first-century historian, tells my all-time favorite tall-tale fishing story. According to him, Marc Antony wanted to impress his mistress, Cleopatra, with his fishing prowess, so he secretly positioned swimmers under their barge to attach fish to his line. At some point the slaves ran out of fresh fish and attached dead salt fish to the line. Cleopatra, who realized what he was doing all along, tactfully reassured Marc Antony to leave fishing to others. "Your game," she said, "is cities, provinces, and kingdoms."

Chapter 4

WATER: SEAFOOD

RED SNAPPER IN PARCHMENT

SEA BASS WITH FETA

GRILLED BASS WITH CORNICHON RELISH

SKATE WITH HERBS AND PECORINO

SHRIMP WITH AROMATIC HERBS

CUMIN-CRUSTED SHARK STEAKS

TUNA WITH MINT-CAPER PESTO

SEARED TUNA WITH ONION-RAISIN MARMALADE

HALIBUT "ALEXANDRIA" WITH PLUM COMPOTE

COD WITH DILL SAUCE

SOLE WITH WALNUTS IN PARCHMENT

SCALLOPS WITH GARLIC CRISPS AND CREAMY ARUGULA

SALMON WITH BERRY GLAZE

RED SNAPPER IN PARCHMENT

Serves 4

This is one of my favorite recipes because it takes only minutes to assemble, can be made hours in advance, and gets rave reviews from guests.

In antiquity, fish was often cooked wrapped in fig leaves and seasoned with just salt and olive oil. This modern version substitutes parchment paper and adds the classic Mediterranean ingredients of capers, olives, lemons, and bay leaves to perfectly season the snapper.

Juice of 2 lemons

2 garlic cloves, minced

$\frac{1}{4}$ cup extra virgin olive oil, plus more as needed

4 bay leaves, crushed

1 $\frac{1}{2}$ teaspoons whole pink peppercorns

2 tablespoons capers, rinsed

15 oil-cured black olives, pitted and halved

4 red snapper fillets, about 8 ounces each

Four 12 by 12-inch parchment sheets

Salt and freshly milled pepper

Lemon wedges

1 Combine the lemon juice, garlic, oil, bay leaves, peppercorns, capers, and olives in a large bowl. Add the red snapper to the marinade, cover with plastic wrap, and refrigerate for at least 2 hours.

2 Preheat the oven to 400° F.

3 Brush both sides of the parchment paper with a little oil. Remove a fillet from the marinade, season with salt and pepper, and place on the paper. Top with several spoonfuls of marinade. To close the packet, bring the top and bottom edges together and fold them over about ½ inch. Continue folding in ½-inch folds until you reach the fillet. Tuck each end of the parchment under the fish. Repeat with the other 3 fillets. Place the parchment packets on a baking sheet.

4 Bake the packets for 10 to 12 minutes. Serve the fish in the paper with the lemon wedges on the side.

THE ANCIENT Romans enjoyed a fermented fish sauce called *garum* or *liquamen*. It was manufactured and distributed throughout the Mediterranean and northern regions of Europe. This all-purpose salty condiment topped everything from vegetables to meats, and was used as we might Worcestershire or soy sauce.

Archaeologists recently excavated an amphora, a large clay vessel, at the site of a Roman ruin in England. The inscription on the outside of the vessel translates as "Seasoned tuna garum, for the pantry, excellent and of high quality."

I experimented with making liquamen from a recipe in an ancient text. It called for several pounds of assorted fish such as smelts and mullet to be covered in salt and left to ferment, uncovered, for two to three months. It is then strained—and, well, I never got that far. After five days my next-door neighbor knocked on my door and sheepishly asked if my cat had died. Since I don't own a cat, I knew the odorous culprit was the liquamen. In the spirit of good neighborliness, I discontinued my fermentation experiment.

There is a form of this fermented fish sauce, called *colatura*, which is still made today in southern Italy. However, if you would like to re-create this basic Roman condiment at home—preferably when the neighbors are on vacation— here is an original Roman recipe.

ORIGINAL RECIPE

Liquamen is made as follows: The entrails of fish are thrown into a vessel and salted. Take small fish, small red mullet or sprats or anchovy or any other small fish, and salt all this together, and leave to dry in the sun, shaking it frequently. When it has become dry from the heat, extract the *garum* from it as follows: Take a long, fine-meshed basket and place it in the middle of the vessel with the above-mentioned fish, and in this way the *liquamen*, put through the basket, can be taken up.

SEA BASS WITH FETA

Serves 4

You cannot teach a crab to walk straight.

—ARISTOPHANES, 450—388 B.C.

This recipe is from the oldest known Greek cookbook, *Art of Cookery*, by Mithaecus. It had a great impact on the foods of Athens and the Greek provinces in the fifth century B.C. Even Plato mentions Mithaecus, noting that he "provided a wonderful service to the body."

The feta and herb topping takes only minutes to assemble, keeps the fish moist, and adds a truly wonderful flavor to bass or your favorite seafood.

$\frac{1}{4}$ cup plain dried bread crumbs

3 ounces feta cheese, crumbled

1 tablespoon olive oil

1 tablespoon minced fresh dill

1 tablespoon minced fresh chives

Salt and freshly milled pepper

4 sea bass fillets, about 7 ounces each

1 Preheat the oven to 375° F.

2 Combine the bread crumbs, cheese, oil, dill, and chives in a small bowl.

3 Generously salt and pepper the bass and place on a lightly greased baking sheet. Press the bread crumb mixture on top of each fillet. Bake, uncovered, until the fish is firm and cooked through, about 20 minutes.

GRILLED BASS WITH CORNICHON RELISH

Serves 4

This sumptuous yet simple-to-prepare cornichon relish was inspired by a cook depicted in a third-century B.C. Greek play. The cook boasts of his skills in quick fish preparation, saying, "What remains to be done? Nothing at all. That is my art."

You'll delight in this unusual creamy relish that is also excellent with shrimp, cod, or even canned tuna.

1 cup sliced European cucumber

1 teaspoon sugar

Salt

1 tablespoon minced fresh parsley

1 tablespoon minced fresh chives

$1\frac{1}{2}$ tablespoons minced shallots

2 teaspoons freshly squeezed lemon juice

8 cornichons, minced

2 tablespoons crème fraîche

1 tablespoon best-quality mayonnaise

2 teaspoons olive oil, plus more as needed

4 bass fillets, about 6 ounces each

Freshly milled pepper

1 Mix the cucumber, sugar, and ½ teaspoon of salt in a small bowl. Allow to rest for 30 minutes, then drain.

2 Puree the cucumber, parsley, chives, shallots, lemon juice, and all but 1 tablespoon of the minced cornichons in a blender or food processor until well combined. Add the crème fraîche, mayonnaise, and oil and pulse until smooth. Place the mixture in a serving bowl and stir in the remaining tablespoon of cornichons. Cover and put in the refrigerator until ready to use.

3 Preheat the grill or broiler. Liberally season the bass with salt and pepper, and lightly brush with oil. Grill or broil until firm, 2 to 3 minutes per side.

4 Serve topped with a dollop of cornichon relish.

SKATE WITH HERBS AND PECORINO

Serves 4

In all things of nature there is something of the marvelous.

—ARISTOTLE, 384—322 B.C.

This dish is accented with fragrant marjoram, an herb that Aristotle believed was an antidote to most poisons.

The original recipe called for ray fish, so I've used skate, a member of the ray family. However, any white-meat fish, such as flounder or sole, can be substituted in this delicious quick-to-prepare recipe.

$1\frac{1}{2}$ cups white wine

2 pounds skinned skate, cut into 4 pieces

Salt and freshly milled pepper

2 tablespoons fresh marjoram leaves, plus sprigs for garnish

3 tablespoons minced assorted fresh herbs, such as parsley, mint, dill, and chives

1 tablespoon extra virgin olive oil

2 tablespoons grated pecorino cheese

1   Bring the wine to a boil in a large skillet over high heat and cook until reduced by half, 5 to 6 minutes. Meanwhile, generously season the fish with salt and pepper.

2   Add the marjoram, minced herbs, and oil to the skillet and mix with the wine. Add the fish and cook, covered, until firm, about 3 minutes.

3   Serve topped with the cheese and a sprig of marjoram.

ORIGINAL RECIPE

And an electric ray stewed in oil and wine, fragrant herbs and a little grated cheese.

—*LIFE OF LUXURY*, ARCHESTRATUS

SHRIMP WITH AROMATIC HERBS

Serves 4

Archestratus, the fourth-century B.C. Greek-Sicilian poet, inspired this dish. His palate was supposedly so refined, he could tell the difference between a fish caught in the waxing moon and one caught in the waning moon.

Archestratus recommends "small fry" in the original recipe. The ancient Greek used the expression "The small fry have seen the fire" for anything done quickly. These delicious shrimp certainly do cook quickly, making this a light and easy-to-prepare starter or main course. Serve them with beans for a classic Mediterranean pairing.

$\frac{1}{3}$ cup extra virgin olive oil

2 garlic cloves, minced

$\frac{3}{4}$ cup assorted fresh aromatic herbs, such as mint, rosemary, sage, and basil

1 bay leaf, crumbled

$1\frac{1}{2}$ pounds medium shrimp, peeled and deveined

Salt and freshly milled pepper

Lemon wedges

1. Puree the oil, garlic, herbs, and bay leaf in a food processor. Place the shrimp in a bowl and toss with this mixture. Cover with plastic wrap and refrigerate for 2 to 3 hours to allow the flavors to mingle.
2. Place the shrimp and herb mixture in a nonstick skillet and cook over medium-high heat until the shrimp are pink and firm, about 1 minute per side. Season to taste with salt and pepper.
3. Serve with lemon wedges.

ORIGINAL RECIPE

Count all small fry as abomination, except the Athenian. . . .
Bake in a pan, after you have made a sauce of the fragrant
tops of choice greens mixed in oil.

— *LIFE OF LUXURY*, ARCHESTRATUS

CUMIN-CRUSTED SHARK STEAKS

Serves 4

Archestratus, the fourth-century B.C. gourmet, advised precisely what time of year was best to catch each type of fish. Since calendars were not standardized in his day, Archestratus gave charming astrological references such as when "the Shining One drives his Chariot to the furthest arc" or when "Orion is setting in the sky."

The cumin and fennel seed crust seals in moistness and adds a marvelous flavor to shark, halibut, or cod. It pairs well with Fennel Salad with Mint Vinaigrette (page 72).

2 tablespoons cumin seeds

2 tablespoons fennel seeds

1 tablespoon whole five-color peppercorns

4 shark or swordfish steaks, about 8 ounces each

Salt

1 tablespoon extra virgin olive oil

Juice and grated zest of 1 lemon

Lemon wedges

1   Preheat the grill or broiler.

2   Grind the cumin, fennel, and peppercorns in a spice grinder. Season the shark with salt and press on the ground spices.

3   Put the shark steaks on the grill and cook until firm, about 3 minutes per side. Arrange on a serving platter topped with a drizzle of the oil, lemon juice, and lemon zest. Serve with lemon wedges.

TUNA WITH MINT-CAPER PESTO

Serves 4

The fourth-century B.C. food writer Archestratus joked that this fish dish is so wonderful, it's impossible to eat slowly, even at the risk of choking. Archestratus, clearly a well-traveled gourmet, made countless references to far-off places as he commented on where to obtain the best ingredients. He rhapsodized about the bread and cake of Athens, the wine of Lesbos, and the exotic products from the Black Sea and Sicily found in Byzantium.

This tantalizing tuna entrée, with just a hint of mint and capers, is light and quick to prepare, perfect for a summer dinner.

1 cup fresh mint leaves

$\frac{1}{3}$ cup capers, drained, plus more for garnish

$\frac{1}{4}$ cup pine nuts, toasted

2 tablespoons freshly squeezed lemon juice

2 tablespoons minced shallots

$\frac{1}{4}$ cup extra virgin olive oil

Salt and freshly milled pepper

4 tuna steaks, $\frac{2}{3}$ inch thick, about 8 ounces each

Lemon wedges

1 Preheat the grill or broiler.

2 Puree the mint, capers, and pine nuts in the bowl of a small food processor until finely ground. Add the lemon juice, shallots, and oil, pulsing several times until well combined. Set aside.

3 Liberally salt and pepper both sides of the tuna steaks. Grill or broil the tuna to the desired doneness, about 2 minutes per side for medium-rare.

4 Top the tuna steaks with a dollop of mint-caper pesto and serve with lemon wedges and a scattering of whole capers.

*To be happy takes a complete lifetime. For one swallow
does not make summer, nor does one fine day; and
similarly one day or a brief period of happiness does
not make a man supremely blessed and happy.*

—ARISTOTLE, 384–322 B.C.

UPON Alexander the Great's birth, King Philip wrote to
Aristotle, "Know that a son is born to me. For this indeed I
thank the gods, not so much because he is born, as because
it is his good fortune to be born during your lifetime." Aristotle tutored Alexander in the standard subjects of the time:
political theory, history, philosophy, and literature.

SEARED TUNA WITH
ONION-RAISIN MARMALADE
Serves 4

Coriander has been cultivated for at least five thousand years. This fragrant spice is mentioned in Sanskrit texts, ancient Egyptian papyri, and even the Bible. The Romans introduced coriander into northern Europe where it was often used to flavor and preserve meats.

This Roman recipe for coriander-crusted tuna with tart-sweet marmalade is also delicious served cold. Leftovers, if there are any, make wonderful sandwiches.

2 large red onions, thinly sliced

1 tablespoon sugar

$\frac{1}{4}$ cup golden raisins

2 tablespoons olive oil

1 tablespoon honey

1 celery rib with leaves, thinly sliced

$\frac{1}{4}$ cup sherry vinegar

Salt and freshly milled pepper

4 tuna steaks, $\frac{1}{2}$ inch thick, about 8 ounces each

$\frac{1}{4}$ cup coriander seeds

2 heaping tablespoons minced fresh parsley

1 Sauté one of the onions, the sugar, and the raisins in the oil in a large nonstick skillet over medium heat until golden, about 10 minutes. Add $\frac{1}{2}$ cup of water and the honey, cover, and simmer for 8 to 10 minutes, until the liquid has evaporated. Add the remaining onion, the celery, and the vinegar. Uncover and simmer for about 4 minutes, until the vinegar has evaporated. Cover once again and simmer for 8 to 10 minutes, until the vegetables are very soft. Season to taste with salt and pepper, and set aside.

2 Preheat the grill or broiler.

3 Liberally season both sides of the tuna with salt and pepper. Coarsely crush the coriander seeds in a sturdy plastic bag using a flat, heavy skillet. Press the crushed seeds on both sides of the tuna steaks.

4 Grill or broil the tuna to the desired doneness, about 2 minutes per side for medium.

5 Arrange the tuna steaks on a serving platter and top with the onion-raisin marmalade and a sprinkle of the parsley.

PLATO, although born into a wealthy aristocratic family, lived very simply, eating only one meal a day. On his return from a visit to lush Sicily, he disapprovingly wrote, "I found myself utterly at odds with the sort of life that is there termed a happy one, a life taken up with Italian and Syracuse banquets, an existence that consists in filling oneself up twice a day, never sleeping alone at night, and indulging in all the practices attendant in that way of living." I don't know about you, but I for one find his description of ancient Sicily rather inviting.

HALIBUT "ALEXANDRIA" WITH PLUM COMPOTE

Serves 4

This recipe was originally named after Alexandria, one of the most important cities and ports in ancient times. Known for its fine fish and other delicacies, Alexandria is often mentioned in Apicius's cookbook, underscoring the connection between Roman and Egyptian cuisine.

The sweet plum compote, an unusually delicious complement to halibut, is also great with sole, flounder, and bass. Toss any leftover compote with canned tuna to make scrumptious luncheon sandwiches.

10 dried plums, chopped

2 teaspoons raspberry or fruit vinegar

4 oil-packed anchovy fillets, drained

3 tablespoons olive oil

2 shallots, sliced

1 leek, white and tender green parts, halved and sliced

$\frac{1}{2}$ teaspoon dried marjoram

$\frac{1}{4}$ teaspoon ground cumin

$\frac{1}{8}$ teaspoon celery seeds

$\frac{1}{4}$ cup red wine

4 halibut steaks, about 8 ounces each

Salt and freshly milled pepper

2 celery ribs with leaves, thinly sliced

1   Toss the plums with the vinegar in a small bowl and set aside.

2   Warm the anchovy fillets in 1 tablespoon of the oil in a saucepan over medium heat, stirring constantly until the fillets are completely broken down. Add the shallots, leek, marjoram, cumin, and celery seeds, and cook until soft, about 5 minutes.

3   Add the wine and simmer until the wine is nearly absorbed. Stir in the vinegar-soaked plums and cook until warmed throughout. Remove from the heat and cover to keep warm while you cook the fish.

4 Season the halibut with salt and pepper. In a large nonstick skillet, heat the remaining 2 tablespoons of oil over medium-high heat. Add the halibut steaks and sauté, turning once, until golden and cooked through, about 4 minutes per side.

5 Stir the celery into the plum-shallot mixture and season to taste with salt and pepper. Serve the halibut topped with several heaping tablespoons of the plum compote.

COD WITH DILL SAUCE

Serves 4

The best Physician is also a Philosopher.

—GALEN, A.D. 129—199

Galen, a second-century physician, was such a prolific writer that his complete works have yet to be fully translated. In one of his books, *On Exercise with the Small Ball*, he recommended sports as an excellent and economical way to stay fit. Homer mentioned ball play as early as the seventh century B.C., and many scholars credit the Spartans as the inventors of ball sports.

Galen considered this sauce the "best for the digestion" but advised that only those in excellent health should eat fried fish. Health benefits aside, this lovely light green sauce looks and tastes so wonderful that it is sure to become one of your favorites.

2 leeks, white and tender green parts, thinly sliced

$\frac{1}{4}$ cup olive oil

1 garlic clove, minced

$\frac{1}{2}$ teaspoon dried savory

$1\frac{1}{2}$ cups chicken stock

$\frac{1}{2}$ cup white wine

1 tablespoon unsalted butter

4 cod fillets, about 8 ounces each

Salt and freshly milled pepper

All-purpose flour for dredging

2 tablespoons minced fresh dill, plus more for garnish

1 Sauté the leeks in 2 tablespoons of the oil in a large skillet over medium heat until soft, 3 to 4 minutes. Add the garlic, savory, stock, and wine, reserving 2 tablespoons of the wine to add later. Raise the heat to high and cook until the liquid has been reduced by half, 12 to 15 minutes.

2 Put the mixture in a food processor, add the butter and reserved wine, and puree. Keep warm while you cook the fish.

3 Liberally season the cod with salt and pepper, and lightly dredge in flour. Heat the remaining 2 tablespoons of oil over high heat in the same skillet. Add the cod fillets and sauté, turning once, until golden, about 2 minutes per side.

4 Arrange the fish on a serving platter. Stir the dill into the sauce and season to taste with salt and pepper. Top the fish with the sauce and garnish with additional dill.

ORIGINAL RECIPE

The recipes which are best for the digestion are made with white sauce. This is how it is made: Put in plenty of water and sufficient olive oil, together with a little dill and leeks. Then reduce the sauce by a half and stir in sufficient salt as not to make the whole sauce too salty.

This recipe is also suitable for those who are ill, whilst fried fish are fine for those who are in perfect health, followed in order by fish baked over a fire. But this recipe requires olive oil and fish-sauce with a little wine, whilst for fried fish it is better to have proportionately more wine and fish-sauce and just a drizzle of olive oil.

—*ON THE POWERS OF FOODS*, BOOK 3, GALEN

SOLE WITH WALNUTS IN PARCHMENT

Serves 4

I was so surprised to discover that fish was cooked in paper two thousand years ago that I spent two days in the library researching the history of paper. I learned that paper as we think of it—made of hardwood pulp—was in fact not readily available until the thirteenth century. However, an inexpensive paper made from the marsh plant papyrus was available then for cooking and wrapping packages sold at market.

Although the original recipe specifies tuna, I prefer the delicate taste of sole with this unusually delicious walnut stuffing.

1 cup shelled walnuts

1 cup fresh parsley leaves

1 cup fresh mint leaves

1 garlic clove, minced

1 tablespoon honey

$\frac{1}{2}$ teaspoon ground cumin

2 tablespoons walnut or olive oil, plus more as needed

Sea salt and freshly milled five-color peppercorns

4 lemon sole fillets, about 8 ounces each

Four 12 by 12-inch sheets of parchment paper

2 tablespoons unsalted butter, softened

Lemon wedges

1   Preheat the oven to 425° F.

2   Finely grind the walnuts in a food processor. Add the parsley, mint, garlic, honey, cumin, oil, $\frac{1}{2}$ teaspoon of salt, and $\frac{1}{4}$ teaspoon of pepper. Puree until well blended.

3   Cut each fillet in half along the natural line in the flesh (one half will be slightly larger). Season with salt and pepper. Divide the walnut stuffing among the fillets and spread it evenly on top. Roll each fillet, enclosing the filling. Put 2 fillet bundles on a sheet of parchment. Dot the top of each fillet with a little butter. To close the packet, bring the top and bottom edges together and fold them over about $\frac{1}{2}$ inch. Continue folding in $\frac{1}{2}$-inch

folds until you reach the fish. Tuck each end of the parchment under the fish. Repeat with the remaining bundles and bake on a baking sheet until cooked through, about 15 minutes.

4   Serve the fish in the parchment paper with a lemon wedge on the side.

ORIGINAL RECIPE

Stuffed bonito. Bone the fish. Pound pennyroyal; add cumin, peppercorns, mint, nuts, honey. Stuff the fish with this mixture and sew up. Wrap in paper and cook in the steam in a covered pan. Season with oil, reduced must [reduced pulp after the wine grapes are mashed], and marjoram.

—*ON COOKERY*, APICIUS

SCALLOPS WITH GARLIC
CRISPS AND CREAMY ARUGULA

Serves 4

Radiant Aphrodite nursed them well on cheese
and luscious honey and heady wine.

—HOMER, CIRCA 700 B.C.

According to Greek myth, Aphrodite, the goddess of love, was carried to the shores of Cyprus in a giant scallop shell. Aphrodite was often associated with the sea, which is perhaps why shellfish is considered an aphrodisiac.

These sweet scallops couple perfectly with the creamy, tart arugula sauce. Although I can't guarantee its aphrodisiac effect, this dish will certainly provoke passionate raves from your guests.

2 cups arugula leaves

1 cup fresh mint leaves

5 tablespoons extra virgin olive oil

$\frac{1}{4}$ cup grated Parmesan cheese

$\frac{1}{4}$ cup heavy cream

Salt and freshly milled pepper

5 garlic cloves, thinly sliced

$1\frac{1}{2}$ pounds large sea scallops

Grated zest of 1 lemon

1   Reserve 1 arugula leaf for garnish. Puree the remaining arugula, the mint, and 3 tablespoons of the oil in a blender until smooth. Add the cheese and blend. Simmer the cream in a small saucepan over medium heat until it begins to boil. With the blender running, drizzle the cream into the arugula puree in a slow stream until well combined. Season to taste with salt and pepper. Cover to keep warm while you cook the scallops.

2   In a large nonstick skillet, warm the remaining 2 tablespoons of oil over medium-high heat. Add the garlic and fry until just golden. Transfer the garlic crisps to a paper towel to

drain. Raise the heat to high. Season the scallops with salt and pepper, and sauté, turning once, until golden, 1 to 2 minutes per side.

3 Slice the reserved arugula leaf into thin ribbons. To serve, pour the arugula puree on 4 serving plates and top with the scallops. Garnish with the garlic crisps, arugula ribbons, and lemon zest.

IN ANTIQUITY, professional cooks hired themselves out for private parties, wedding feasts, and other special occasions. Cooks were often featured as comical characters in plays, poems, and other literature. In one Greek comedy a cook playfully boasts, "I have found the elixir of life: men already dead, once they but catch a whiff from my food, come back to life."

Hired cooks were notorious not only for their conceit but also for their dishonesty. A centuries-old comedy about a chef who boasts of his kitchen thievery was found among papyrus fragments in Alexandria: "They numbered off the slices of meat for me: I made them smaller, but the same in number. There was some tripe on a spit: I took three cuts out of the middle, and then brought the ends together. . . . There was some cheese: I grabbed it. . . . I took honey along with me. There was some silphium left over, juice, cumin, mustard: I took a sponge, stuffed it full of them, and carried it away."

SALMON WITH BERRY GLAZE
Serves 4

Love conquers all things; let us too surrender to Love.
—VIRGIL, 70–19 B.C.

Naturally sweet seared salmon is topped with a slightly tart mulberry sauce to create this delectable dish inspired by Stodes, a third-century B.C. Athenian poet. Raspberries are a wonderful substitute if you don't have access to a mulberry bush.

The ancients created a myth about how mulberries got their deep red color: Two lovers, prevented from marrying by their families, arranged to meet near a mulberry tree late one night. When the girl's lover came to the appointed spot, he mistakenly thought she was dead and, in despair, killed himself. When the girl arrived a few minutes later, she realized her lover's mistake and killed herself, too.

The gods immortalized the young couple's devotion to each other by turning the white fruit of the nearby mulberry tree red in honor of their love.

2 tablespoons unsalted butter

2 medium shallots, minced

$\frac{1}{2}$ cup raspberry vinegar

$\frac{1}{2}$ pint fresh mulberries or raspberries, plus more for garnish

1 teaspoon honey

Salt and crushed red peppercorns

4 salmon steaks or fillets, about 6 ounces each

1 tablespoon olive oil

1   Melt 1 tablespoon of the butter in a small saucepan over low heat. Add the shallots and cook for 3 to 4 minutes, or until translucent. Add the vinegar, raise the heat to medium-high, and boil for 1 minute to reduce the acidity. Lower the heat to medium, add the berries, and cook until thick, about 15 minutes. Strain, pressing the solids to remove all the liquid, and return the liquid to the saucepan. Simmer for about 5 minutes to thicken, then whisk in the remaining tablespoon of butter and the honey over low heat. Season to taste with salt and pepper. Keep warm.

2   Liberally season the salmon with salt and pepper. Heat the oil in a large nonstick skillet

over medium-high heat. Add the salmon and cook until golden, 2 to 3 minutes per side for steaks or about 4 minutes per side for fillets.

3 Arrange the salmon on a serving platter. Serve with the berry glaze and garnish with additional whole berries and crushed red pepper.

ORIGINAL RECIPE

A huge dog-fish [a type of small shark, also referred to as a rock salmon] is put in my hands; I baked the middle slices, but the rest of the stuff I boiled, after making a mulberry sauce.

—"LOCKED UP," STODES,
IN *THE PHILOSOPHER'S BANQUET*, ATHENAEUS

THE ANCIENT Romans enjoyed a wide variety of fowl, including ostrich, peacock, turtledove, crane, pigeon, pheasant, duck, and goose.

During Caesar's reign several laws were enacted regulating feasts, specifying types of foods permitted, maximum number of guests allowed, and even how much silverware could be on the table at one time.

The laws mandated that the only fowl allowed at feasts were hens, and they even further ruled that hens could not be fattened by forced feedings. The law was universally hated because hens, which could produce eggs, were butchered while the otherwise unproductive roosters were spared. Some scholars believe that the capon was created as a way to bypass these laws. Capons, which are castrated roosters, could be fattened and eaten at feasts without breaking any rules because they were not, strictly speaking, hens or roosters.

Chapter 5

AIR: POULTRY

SEARED DUCK BREAST WITH GLAZED TURNIPS

ROAST CHICKEN WITH OLIVE STUFFING

CHICKEN WITH PLUMS

MARINATED CHICKEN WITH DATE MUSTARD

CORNISH GAME HENS
WITH DRIED FRUIT STUFFING

CHICKEN BREASTS WITH HAZELNUT PESTO

BRAISED CHICKEN WITH PEACHES AND SQUASH

GRAPES-AND-COUSCOUS-STUFFED CHICKEN BREASTS

MARJORAM CHICKEN

CHICKEN FROM ANCIENT AFRICA

CHICKEN WITH LEEK SAUCE

SEARED DUCK BREAST WITH GLAZED TURNIPS

Serves 2

I was surprised to find a recipe for duck with turnips in an almost two-thousand-year-old Roman cookery book. I had always thought the combination of crisp duck and sweet roasted turnips was a traditional French innovation called *canard aux navets*, duck with turnips.

I like duck but dread the mess of roasting a whole one in the oven. By buying just the breast portion, which cooks beautifully in a skillet on the stovetop, I get my favorite slices of meat and avoid the oven altogether. One taste and you'll know why this recipe has been around for two millennia.

1 duck breast, about 1 pound

Salt and freshly milled pepper

2 white turnips, quartered and cut into $1/4$-inch slices

1 leek, white and tender green parts, thinly sliced

$1/3$ cup muscatel or sherry vinegar

$1/3$ cup chicken stock

$1/4$ teaspoon dried thyme

$1/2$ teaspoon dried dill

1   Liberally season the duck with salt and pepper, and pierce the skin in several places with a fork. In a medium skillet, cook the duck, skin side down, over very low heat until it is dark brown and crispy, 15 to 17 minutes. Drain the fat from the pan periodically as it cooks. Remove the duck from the pan, leaving 1 tablespoon of fat.

2   Add the turnips and cook in the fat over high heat until golden, about 3 minutes. Add the leek and vinegar, stirring to loosen the pan drippings, and cook until the vinegar has almost evaporated, about 3 minutes. Add the stock, thyme, and dill, and bring to a boil.

3   Adjust the heat to low and return the duck to the pan, skin side up. Cover and cook until the turnips are tender, 5 to 8 minutes.

4   Remove the duck from the pan. Season the turnips to taste with salt and pepper. Cut the duck into thin slices and arrange the slices in the center of each plate, surrounded by the turnips.

ORIGINAL RECIPE

Crane or duck with turnips. Wash and truss the bird and boil it in a large saucepan in water, salt, and dill, until half done. Cook the turnips so that they lose their pungency. Remove the duck from the pan, wash again, and put into another saucepan with oil, liquamen [fermented fish sauce], and a bouquet of leek and coriander. Put over it one washed and finely snipped turnip, and braise. When it has been cooking for a while, add reduced wine to give it color. Then prepare the following sauce: pepper, cumin, coriander, asafetida root; add vinegar and some of the cooking liquid; pour over the duck and bring to a boil. When it boils, thicken with flour and add to the turnips. Sprinkle with pepper and serve.

—*ON COOKERY*, APICIUS

ROAST CHICKEN
WITH OLIVE STUFFING
Serves 4

In the original recipe, chicken was stuffed with olives and taro, suspended in a tight-fitting basket, and boiled. Since taro, a potato-like tuber, is hard to find, I've substituted baby red potatoes. I've also changed the cooking technique from boiling to roasting for crisper skin. The resulting golden chicken with olive and potato stuffing is an unusually tasty entrée. Adding carrots and other root vegetables during roasting makes this a one-pan, easy-to-prepare complete meal.

$\frac{1}{4}$ cup extra virgin olive oil

2 garlic cloves, minced

2 long sprigs fresh rosemary

$1\frac{1}{2}$ pounds baby red potatoes, unpeeled

$\frac{1}{3}$ cup minced oil-cured black olives

$\frac{1}{3}$ cup minced green olives

1 large red onion, thinly sliced

$\frac{1}{2}$ cup minced fresh parsley

Salt and freshly milled pepper

1 roasting chicken, about 5 pounds

Assorted root vegetables, cut into chunks

1   Mix the oil with half of the minced garlic and the rosemary in a small jar or bowl. Allow the flavors to mingle overnight or while you prepare the other ingredients.

2   Boil 4 or 5 of the potatoes in a small saucepan until tender, about 10 minutes. Dice them (you should get about $1\frac{1}{4}$ cups) and mix with the olives in a medium-sized bowl.

3   Preheat the oven to 425° F.

4   Sauté the onion in 2 tablespoons of the garlic oil in a small skillet over medium heat until golden, about 8 minutes. Add with the parsley to the potato-olive mixture. Stir in the remaining minced garlic and season to taste with salt and pepper.

5   Liberally season the chicken with salt and pepper inside and out and place in a greased baking pan. Drizzle the remaining garlic oil on the skin. Insert the rosemary branches into the cavity and fill with the potato-olive mixture.

6 Bake for 30 minutes, lower the heat to 375° F, and add the remaining uncooked potatoes and root vegetables to the pan. Continue to bake for another 30 to 40 minutes, or until the skin is golden brown and the juices run clear when the chicken leg is pierced with a fork.

7 Arrange the chicken on a serving platter and surround with the roasted potatoes and vegetables.

INTERESTINGLY, Hippocrates gave advice for losing weight that sounds surprisingly like the low-carbohydrate diets so popular today. The Father of Medicine wrote, "People who wish to become thin should . . . let the foods be rich. For so the appetite will be satisfied with a minimum." Hippocrates realized two thousand years ago what modern physicians are only recently advocating: that a diet rich in fats and proteins can reduce cravings and decrease appetite, resulting in weight loss.

CHICKEN WITH PLUMS

Serves 4

Medicine is the most distinguished of all the arts, but through the ignorance of those who practice it, and of those who casually judge such practitioners, it is now of all the arts by far the least esteemed.

—HIPPOCRATES, 460—377 B.C.

For optimum health and digestion Hippocrates recommended that fruit be eaten often, especially with meats. This recipe calls for plums, which in antiquity came from Africa, Asia, or Damascus and were distributed fresh or preserved in honey or wine.

Plums and chicken are a wonderful taste combination, so you'll want to serve this succulent dish over rice or couscous to get every drop of sweet and silky sauce.

4 skinless and boneless chicken breasts, about $1\frac{1}{2}$ pounds

Salt and freshly milled pepper

All-purpose flour for dredging

3 tablespoons extra virgin olive oil

1 large red onion, thinly sliced

1 celery rib, thinly sliced

1 teaspoon ground cumin

$\frac{1}{2}$ teaspoon celery seeds

2 plums, pitted and thinly sliced

$\frac{1}{2}$ cup sweet sherry

$\frac{3}{4}$ cup chicken stock

1   Cut the chicken breasts into $\frac{1}{2}$-inch-wide strips. Liberally salt and pepper them, and dredge in flour. In a large skillet, warm 2 tablespoons of the oil over high heat and cook the chicken on all sides until golden, about 2 minutes per side. Remove the chicken from the skillet, cover to keep warm, and set aside.

2   Lower the heat to medium and add the remaining tablespoon of oil and the onion, celery, cumin, and celery seeds. Cook until the onion is translucent, about 3 minutes. Add the plums and sherry, stirring to loosen the pan drippings, and cook for 3 minutes, or until the sherry has almost evaporated.

3   Add the stock and bring to a boil. Adjust the heat to very low and return the chicken to the pan. Cover and cook until the chicken is cooked through, about 5 minutes. Serve warm.

ORIGINAL RECIPE

For crane, duck, or chicken. Pepper, shallots, lovage, cumin, celery seed, Damascus plums stones removed, reduced wine, vinegar, liquamen [fermented fish sauce], reduced wine, and oil. Cook.

—*ON COOKERY*, APICIUS

IN ANTIQUITY, philosophers considered it a virtue to take care of one's body, which was evidence of self-control and discipline. Philosophers even addressed exercise regimens and healthful eating for athletes. Aristotle observed the differences between proper nutrition for beginning athletes and those who were advanced. Plato noted that sugar should be avoided by all athletes, saying, "all men in training understand—that if one is to keep his body in good condition, he must abstain from such things all together."

MARINATED CHICKEN WITH DATE MUSTARD

Serves 4

This easy-to-make mustard is outstanding, a perfect partner for this tangy marinated chicken and also wonderful with burgers or grilled vegetables.

It is fitting that this mustard dish was found in an ancient Roman cookbook because the word *mustard* comes from Latin, a combination of *mustum*, reduced pulp after the wine grapes are mashed, and *ardens*, fiery hot.

$\frac{1}{4}$ cup white wine vinegar

$\frac{1}{4}$ cup plus $\frac{1}{3}$ cup extra virgin olive oil

Salt

$\frac{1}{2}$ teaspoon dry mustard

Freshly milled pepper

$\frac{1}{4}$ teaspoon celery seeds

2 celery ribs, minced

4 chicken legs with thighs attached

$\frac{1}{4}$ cup sliced pitted dates

2 tablespoons cider vinegar

1 tablespoon prepared whole-grain mustard

1   Whisk together the white wine vinegar, $\frac{1}{4}$ cup of oil, 1 teaspoon of the salt, the dry mustard, and $\frac{1}{4}$ teaspoon of pepper in a large bowl until combined. Stir in the celery seeds and minced celery. Add the chicken legs to the marinade and toss until well coated. Cover and refrigerate for at least 2 hours for the flavors to mingle.

2   Meanwhile, puree the dates, the remaining $\frac{1}{3}$ cup of oil, cider vinegar, the prepared mustard, $\frac{1}{2}$ teaspoon of salt, and $\frac{1}{4}$ cup of water in a food processor until smooth. Transfer to a small saucepan and warm over low heat. Set aside.

3   Preheat an outdoor gas grill to medium heat or prepare a charcoal grill. When the grill is ready, remove the chicken from the marinade and grill, turning, until all sides are dark golden and cooked through, about 8 minutes per side. During the last few minutes of cooking, brush the chicken with a small amount of the warm date mustard.

4   Serve hot with additional date mustard on the side.

ORIGINAL RECIPE

Another sauce [for wood pigeons and pigeons]. Boiled.
Pepper, caraway, celery seed, parsley, the spices you use
for moretum [herbs such as mint, rue, coriander, fennel,
and lovage pounded in a mortar], Jericho date, honey,
vinegar, wine, oil, and mustard.

— ON COOKERY, APICIUS

CORNISH GAME HENS
WITH DRIED FRUIT STUFFING
Serves 2

All art is but imitation of nature.

—SENECA THE YOUNGER, 4 B.C.—A.D. 65

As the story goes, two rival fourth-century B.C. artists competed to paint the most realistic-looking still life. One painted a cluster of grapes so lifelike that birds swooped down to peck at it. Pleased with this obvious proof of his realism, the painter asked his rival to take the curtain off his canvas. Realizing that he had been tricked by the "curtain," which was actually the rival's painting, the artist conceded victory to his rival.

This moist and sweet fruit stuffing makes for a picture-perfect meal.

2 Cornish game hens

Salt and freshly milled pepper

1 tablespoon unsalted butter, melted

1 small onion, diced

1 celery rib with leaves, diced

2 tablespoons olive oil

$\frac{1}{3}$ cup diced dried plums

$\frac{1}{4}$ cup golden raisins

$\frac{1}{4}$ cup sweet sherry

$\frac{1}{4}$ cup chicken stock

$1\frac{1}{4}$ cups cubed crusty country bread

1   Season the game hens' skin and cavities with salt and pepper. Brush the skin with the butter.
2   Preheat the oven to 375° F.
3   Sauté the onion and celery in the oil in a large saucepan over medium heat until soft, about 6 minutes. Raise the heat to high; add the plums, raisins, and sherry; and cook until the fruit is soft, 2 to 3 minutes. Add the stock, remove from the heat, and fold in the bread cubes. Season with salt and pepper, and spoon the stuffing into the hens.

4 Place the hens in a lightly buttered roasting pan and bake until golden and the leg juices run clear when pierced with a fork, about 1 hour. Baste with the pan juices every 10 minutes.

5 Place the hens on plates and serve.

Imitation is the sincerest of flattery.
—CHARLES CALEB COLTON, 1780–1832

CLASSICAL Greek art and sculpture was much appreciated and heavily copied by the Romans. The first to develop private art collections, Romans began in the third century B.C. to acquire Greek art to decorate their villas. Many Greek artists migrated to Rome, fulfilling the huge demand for fine objects there, and it was during this period that Europe's first public art gallery was created.

Works such as the *Venus de Milo*, the *Winged Victory*, and the Elgin Marbles continue to awe modern audiences.

CHICKEN BREASTS
WITH HAZELNUT PESTO
Serves 4

It is impossible to live pleasurably without living wisely, well, and justly,
and impossible to live wisely, well, and justly without living pleasurably.
—EPICURUS, 341–270 B.C.

This recipe, originally titled Chicken Varius, was probably named after the Epicurean poet Varius Rufus. One of Varius's poems concerns the Epicurean belief that the only reality is the present moment and that the future holds nothing to fear.

This extraordinary rich hazelnut pesto will please any modern-day epicure. For variety, try it with almonds or walnuts.

4 bone-in chicken breast halves, skin on

Salt and freshly milled pepper

All-purpose flour for dredging

$\frac{1}{4}$ cup olive oil

1 leek, white and tender green parts, thinly sliced

$\frac{1}{2}$ teaspoon ground coriander

$\frac{1}{2}$ teaspoon dried savory

$1\frac{1}{2}$ cups white wine

$\frac{3}{4}$ cup chicken stock

$\frac{1}{2}$ cup blanched hazelnuts, plus 2 tablespoons for garnish

$\frac{1}{2}$ cup whole milk

2 tablespoons minced fresh chives

Grated zest of 1 lemon

1 Season the chicken breasts generously with salt and pepper, and dredge them in flour.

2 In a nonstick skillet large enough to hold all 4 breasts, warm the oil over high heat. When the oil is hot but not smoking, add the chicken breasts, skin side down. Brown the skin to a dark golden color, turn, and brown the underside. Remove the chicken to a platter and cover to keep warm. Lower the heat to medium.

3 Add the leek, coriander, and savory to the skillet and sauté until the leek is softened, about 2 minutes. Add the wine and simmer until the wine is reduced by half. Add the stock and return the chicken, skin side up, to the pan. Cover with a tight-fitting lid and simmer until the chicken is cooked through, about 25 minutes.

4 Meanwhile, toast the hazelnuts in a nonstick skillet, stirring frequently, until golden. Once cool, grind them in a food processor. Reserve 2 tablespoons for the garnish.

5 Remove the chicken from the skillet. Put all the pan liquids into the food processor with the ground hazelnuts and add the milk. Puree until smooth.

6 Pour the sauce on a serving platter, place the chicken on top, and garnish with the reserved hazelnuts, the chives, and the lemon zest.

EPICURUS, born in 341 B.C., founded a school of philosophy that admitted as students not only free men but also slaves and even women. Epicurus and his followers engaged in philosophical discussions while actively but tactfully avoiding any involvement in politics.

According to Epicurus, the main purpose of philosophy was teaching man that "pleasure is the beginning and end of living happily."

The Epicureans valued friendship and developed long-lasting and deep ties with one another. To commemorate his birthday, Epicurus left funds and instructions in his will for an annual banquet to be enjoyed by his followers and friends.

BRAISED CHICKEN
WITH PEACHES AND SQUASH

Serves 4

You will eat them [squash] first as appetizer;
He will serve them in the first and second courses,
And place them before you again in the third;
Then he will prepare dessert from them.
And afterward his baker will use them
To make sweet focaccias.

—MARTIAL, A.D. 40—103

As we read in this poem by Martial, squash was one of the most popular and frequently served Roman vegetables. In the original recipe, squash was combined with peaches and truffles to create a succulent sauce for poultry. However, the wonderful blending of squash and sweet peaches tastes quite rich enough without truffles.

4 chicken legs and thighs, separated

Salt and freshly milled pepper

All-purpose flour for dredging

2 tablespoons extra virgin olive oil

1 teaspoon caraway seeds

$1\frac{1}{2}$ teaspoons ground cumin

1 acorn squash, halved, seeded, and sliced $\frac{1}{2}$ inch thick

2 cups white wine

1 firm peach, pitted and thinly sliced

2 tablespoons minced fresh cilantro

2 tablespoons minced watercress

Grated black truffle (optional)

1   Liberally season the chicken with salt and pepper, and dredge in flour. In a large sauté pan, warm the oil over high heat and brown the chicken on all sides. Remove the chicken

and all but 3 tablespoons of the juices from the pan. Add the caraway seeds, cumin, and squash, and cook until golden, 2 to 3 minutes.

2   Add the wine to the squash and bring to a boil. Return the chicken to the pan, cover with a tight lid, and adjust the heat to low. Simmer, stirring occasionally, for 30 minutes, or until the chicken is cooked through.

3   Remove the chicken and squash from the pan and arrange on a serving platter. Add the sliced peach to the pan juices and simmer for 5 to 10 minutes, or until the liquid has reduced by half. Remove from the heat. Stir in the cilantro and watercress, and then pour the liquid over the chicken and squash. Serve topped with grated truffle, if using.

ORIGINAL RECIPE

Pumpkin and Fowl. Peaches, truffles, caraway, cumin, asafetida, mixed fresh herbs—mint, celery, coriander, and pennyroyal—reduced wine, honey, wine, liquamen [fermented fish sauce], oil, and vinegar.

— *ON COOKERY*, APICIUS

GRAPES-AND-COUSCOUS-STUFFED CHICKEN BREASTS

Serves 4

One swallow does not make a summer.

—ARISTOTLE, 384—322 B.C.

This dish is inspired by a summer meal described by Artemidorus, a second-century B.C. Greek writer. He mentioned that it should be brought in on "the second table," meaning the second course, as each course was set before guests on a different portable table.

This succulent stuffed chicken breast, also wonderful served cold, transports easily to make for perfect summer picnicking. You'll love how attractive it looks when sliced.

1 tablespoon unsalted butter

Salt

$\frac{1}{2}$ cup dried instant couscous

$1\frac{1}{4}$ cups green seedless grapes, halved

1 celery rib, finely minced

2 teaspoons chopped fresh parsley

1 teaspoon chopped fresh mint

4 boneless chicken breast halves, skin on

Freshly milled pepper

$1\frac{1}{2}$ cups white wine

$\frac{1}{2}$ cup sliced blanched almonds, toasted, plus more for garnish

1 tablespoon chopped fresh chives, plus more for garnish

1. Bring the butter, $\frac{1}{2}$ teaspoon of salt, and $\frac{1}{2}$ cup of water to a boil in a small saucepan. Remove from the heat and add the couscous. Cover and allow to stand for 5 minutes. Uncover, fluff with a fork, and mix in $\frac{1}{2}$ cup of grapes, celery, parsley, and mint.

2. Preheat the oven to 400° F.

3. On a work surface, butterfly each chicken breast and pound to $\frac{1}{4}$ inch thick. Season both sides with salt and pepper. Divide the couscous mixture evenly among the breasts and roll them to enclose the stuffing. Lay them, seam side down, in a well-greased baking

pan. Bake, uncovered, on the center rack of the oven until the chicken is cooked through, about 30 minutes.

4   Meanwhile, bring the wine, the remaining ¾ cup of grapes, and the almonds to a boil in a medium saucepan over high heat. Cook until reduced by two-thirds, about 10 minutes. Remove from the heat and allow to cool slightly. Transfer to a blender, add the chives and ¼ teaspoon of salt, and puree until smooth.

5   Serve the stuffed chicken breasts sliced with the green grape sauce poured over the top. Garnish with the chives and almonds.

EXERCISING in the town gymnasium or public baths was part of everyday Greek life. According to Hippocrates, "Walking is a natural exercise, much more so than other exercises"; however, running was probably the Greeks' preferred sport. They ran on circular running tracks for long-distance training and on what Hippocrates called a "double track" for sprinting.

I chuckled at Hippocrates' advice for those with sore, overworked muscles: "Get drunk once or twice" and have "sexual intercourse after a moderate indulgence in wine."

MARJORAM CHICKEN
Serves 4

The goddess Aphrodite created the sweet scent of marjoram as a symbol of happiness, and traditionally brides wore crowns of fresh wild marjoram, an herb which grew in the hills throughout Greece. In fact, marjoram and oregano, both in the same herb family, were named *oros ganos*, joy of the mountain by the ancient Greeks.

Instead of thickening the sauce with "crumbled pastry," as directed in the original recipe, the creamy marjoram-scented chicken is topped with toasted bread crumbs for color and crunch. This must-try recipe is sure to bring joy to your table.

1 large onion, diced

2 tablespoons olive oil

$\frac{1}{2}$ cup white wine

1 cup chicken stock

1 teaspoon ground coriander

4 skinless and boneless chicken breasts, 6 ounces each

Salt and freshly milled five-color peppercorns

1 cup half-and-half

1 tablespoon honey

2 tablespoons dried marjoram

3 tablespoons plain dried bread crumbs, toasted

1 Sauté the onion in the oil in a large sauté pan over medium-high heat until golden, about 8 minutes. Add the wine and simmer until reduced, 3 to 4 minutes. Add the stock and coriander, and bring to a boil.

2 Liberally season the chicken with salt and pepper. Lower the heat to medium, add the chicken to the pan, and cover tightly. Allow the chicken to simmer in the liquid, turning once, until cooked through, about 4 minutes per side.

3 Meanwhile, in a small saucepan over very low heat, simmer the half-and-half, the honey, and 1 tablespoon of the marjoram until the liquid is reduced by half, 12 to 15 minutes.

4 Remove the chicken from the cooking liquid, place on a plate, and cover to keep warm. Raise the heat to high and boil the cooking liquid until reduced by half, about 5 minutes. Add the half-and-half mixture to the cooking liquid and stir to combine. Season to taste with salt and pepper.

5   Pour the sauce on a serving platter and top with the chicken. Sprinkle with the bread crumbs and the remaining tablespoon of marjoram, and serve immediately.

THE GREAT philosopher Socrates never wrote about philosophy—not one book, not one essay, not one line. He considered the written word inferior to the spoken word, so we learn of his teachings only through the works of pupils and friends such as Plato, Aristophanes, Xenophon, and others.

Gellius, the second-century historian, noted that Socrates lived a long and illness-free life, probably due to his disciplined drinking and eating habits. To develop self-control, Socrates would spend an entire day, "from early dawn until the next sunrise, open-eyed, motionless, in his very tracks and with face and eyes riveted to the same spot in meditation."

CHICKEN FROM ANCIENT AFRICA

Serves 6

There is always something new out of Africa.

—PLINY THE ELDER, A.D. 23–79

This Roman recipe was originally named for Numidia, a region in ancient Africa. This small territory, from the Atlas Mountains to the border of the Sahara, supplied Rome with such agricultural products as wine, wheat, and olives. It was also Rome's main source of marble and wild animals, including bears, lions, leopards, and elephants, for amphitheater events.

The unusual aromatic combination of sweet and spicy flavors is perfect for serving with saffron rice or Crisp Chickpea Wedges (page 174).

$\frac{1}{2}$ cup all-purpose flour

1 teaspoon ground coriander

Freshly milled five-color peppercorns

$\frac{1}{2}$ teaspoon ground cloves

$\frac{1}{2}$ teaspoon ground cinnamon

$\frac{1}{2}$ teaspoon ground allspice

$\frac{1}{2}$ teaspoon ground cumin

4 skinless and boneless chicken breasts, about $1\frac{1}{2}$ pounds, cubed

Salt

$\frac{1}{4}$ cup walnut or olive oil

2 cups chicken stock

$\frac{1}{4}$ cup white wine vinegar

$\frac{1}{2}$ cup chopped pitted dates

1 tablespoon honey

1 teaspoon Worcestershire sauce

1 teaspoon bottled horseradish

4 ounces bitter greens, such as arugula, mustard greens, or
    dandelion greens, chopped

2 tablespoons chopped fresh cilantro

1 Preheat the oven to 375° F.

2 Mix the flour, ½ teaspoon of the coriander, ½ teaspoon of the pepper, cloves, cinnamon, allspice, and cumin in a large bowl. Season the chicken generously with salt and pepper. Toss the chicken in the seasoned flour until well coated. Discard any excess flour.

3 Heat the oil in a large Dutch oven over medium-high heat. Add the chicken and brown on all sides, about 4 minutes per side. Transfer the chicken to a plate. Add the stock and vinegar to the pan and bring to a boil, scraping up any browned bits at the bottom of the pan. Stir in the remaining ½ teaspoon of coriander, ½ teaspoon of pepper, and the dates, honey, Worcestershire, and horseradish. Stir in the chicken, cover, and bake until the sauce is thick and bubbly, 30 to 35 minutes.

4 Remove from the oven, mix in the greens and cilantro, and serve.

ORIGINAL RECIPE

Chicken in the Numidian Way. Prepare the chicken, boil, take out, sprinkle with asafetida and pepper, and roast. Pound pepper, cumin, coriander seed, asafetida root, rue, Jericho date, pine nuts; moisten with vinegar, honey, liquamen [fermented fish sauce], and oil. Mix well. When it boils, thicken with flour, pour over the chicken, sprinkle with pepper, and serve.

—ON COOKERY, APICIUS

CHICKEN WITH LEEK SAUCE
Serves 4

Very little is needed to make a happy life.
—MARCUS AURELIUS, A.D. 121—180

This dish, from a first-century Roman cookbook, was originally named after Marcus Fronto, much-loved tutor to the emperor and philosopher Marcus Aurelius, who taught that life's essentials are often very simple.

This simple but marvelous leek sauce accented with dill is perfect with chicken and also lovely with your favorite seafood.

4 skinless and boneless chicken breasts

Salt and freshly milled pepper

$\frac{1}{4}$ cup olive oil

2 leeks, white and tender green parts, thinly sliced

2 garlic cloves, minced

$\frac{1}{2}$ teaspoon dried savory

$\frac{1}{2}$ cup white wine

1 cup chicken stock

2 heaping tablespoons minced fresh dill

1 Liberally season the chicken with salt and pepper. Heat the oil in a large skillet over medium-high heat and sear both sides of the chicken, about 1 minute per side. Remove the chicken from the skillet, cover to keep warm, and set aside.

2 In the same pan over medium heat, sauté the leeks until soft, about 3 minutes. Add the garlic, savory, wine, and stock, and bring to a boil. Lower the heat, add the chicken, cover, and cook for about 3 minutes. Turn and cook the other side until the juices run clear when the chicken is pierced with a fork.

3 Top the chicken with the sauce and garnish with the dill.

THE ANCIENT Greeks and Romans rarely ate beef,

since the rocky Mediterranean region made raising

cattle difficult. Instead, goat, rabbit, deer, and

especially pork were more common meats.

Whole roast pig was a favorite Roman celebratory

dish. The pig or boar was stuffed with a large fowl that

had also been stuffed with progressively smaller birds,

each containing its own different grain or fruit filling.

Chapter 6

MACELLUM: MEATS

MEATBALLS IN POMEGRANATE SAUCE

PORK CHOPS SIMMERED WITH TWO WINES

SEARED STEAK WITH FIG GLAZE

SAVORY PORK-FILLED ACORN SQUASH

PORK LOIN WITH APPLES AND PANCETTA

GINGERSNAP-CRUSTED PORK LOIN
WITH BRANDIED FIG SAUCE

LAMB WITH POMEGRANATE-GLAZED ONIONS

VEAL CHOPS WITH QUINCE AND LEEKS

MARINATED BEEF TENDERLOIN WITH CUCUMBER-ONION RELISH

SEASONED SALT

MEATBALLS IN POMEGRANATE SAUCE

Serves 4

One good turn deserves another.

—PETRONIUS, D. A.D. 66

Petronius, Nero's friend, wrote a satire on life in imperial Rome aptly entitled the *Satyricon*. One chapter details a dinner party where platter after platter of progressively outlandish dishes was served. Among the many offerings—ironically intended to point to excess—was one that inspired this recipe. Meat tidbits were served on a silver grill "while beneath black damson plums and red pomegranates had been sliced and arranged so as to give the effect of flames playing over charcoal."

Plums and pomegranates not only look whimsically like flames on charcoal, but together they also create a delicious sauce that has the perfect mix of sweet and tart.

1 pound ground pork or beef

2 tablespoons plain dried bread crumbs

1 tablespoon dried oregano

2 tablespoons minced fresh mint

3 tablespoons minced fresh parsley

$\frac{1}{4}$ teaspoon fennel seeds

1 large egg

3 tablespoons minced shallots

Salt and freshly milled pepper

2 tablespoons olive oil

1 cup red wine

1 pomegranate

$\frac{1}{4}$ teaspoon ground nutmeg

1 bay leaf

$\frac{1}{4}$ cup beef stock

1 plum, pitted and thinly sliced

1   Mix the ground pork with the bread crumbs, oregano, mint, parsley, fennel seeds, egg, shallots, $\frac{1}{2}$ teaspoon of salt, and $\frac{1}{4}$ teaspoon of pepper in a large bowl. Form $1\frac{1}{2}$-inch meatballs.

2   In a large nonstick skillet, fry the meatballs in the oil over medium heat, turning them so that they cook on all sides. Remove the meatballs from the skillet and cover to keep warm while you make the pomegranate sauce.

3   Add the wine to the skillet and bring to a boil and boil until reduced by half, about 5 minutes.

4   Cut the pomegranate in half and reserve 2 tablespoons of seeds. Very gently squeeze each half of the pomegranate until you get $\frac{1}{4}$ cup of juice. Add it to the skillet with the nutmeg, bay leaf, stock, and plum slices. Continue to cook on high until the plum slices are soft, 3 to 4 minutes. Return the meatballs to the pan and toss with the sauce. Season with salt and pepper. Top with pomegranate seeds and serve immediately.

THE *SATYRICON* provides a glimpse into the everyday lives of the upper classes in imperial Rome. We learn that the Romans enjoyed aged wine—"Just think, friends, wine lasts longer than us poor suffering humans"—used silver toothpicks, and had their hands washed by slaves as they entered the feasting room. We discover that table talk included riddles, jokes, and puns, and unlike the Greeks, the Romans dined with their wives.

From the guests' dinner conversation we learn that the ancient Romans believed in the existence of werewolves, cooks were often slaves, the host gave his guests parting gifts such as jars of perfume, and for many the philosophy was "We all have to die, so let's live while we're waiting!"

Trimalchio, an ex-slave who became wealthy, was eager to impress his guests and served fanciful dishes such as egg-shaped pastry filled with seasoned fowl and a Pegasus rabbit roasted with pastry wings. To amuse his guests Trimalchio served a tray of twelve different foods to represent the twelve signs of the zodiac. For example, Taurus was represented by slices of beef; Gemini, a pair of sweetbreads; Scorpio, a crawfish; and Pisces, two mullet.

PORK CHOPS SIMMERED WITH TWO WINES

Serves 4

Show your grapes to the sun for ten days and for ten nights.
Cover them with shade for five, and on the sixth day,
press out the gifts of bountiful Dionysus into jars.

—HESIOD, CIRCA 800 B.C.

The ancients cooked using several types of wine in one recipe, including spiced wines and reduced wine syrup. Popular was "raisin wine," or late-harvest wine, made from grapes allowed to dry on the vine. These naturally sweet wines, such as Italy's Passito and France's Vin de Paille, are still available today.

The sauce from this double-wine recipe is outstanding, so be sure to serve it with lots of bread to savor every drop.

1 cup white wine

3 shallots, sliced

1 celery rib, thinly sliced

$\frac{1}{2}$ teaspoon celery seeds

3 tablespoons extra virgin olive oil

4 pork chops, bone in, about 8 ounces each

Salt and freshly milled pepper

$\frac{1}{4}$ cup dessert wine

3 heaping tablespoons chopped fresh celery leaves

1 Bring the white wine to a simmer in a small saucepan over medium heat and simmer until reduced by half, about 10 minutes. Reserve.

2 Sauté the shallots, celery, and celery seeds in the oil in a large skillet over medium heat until the shallots are translucent, 2 to 3 minutes.

3 Liberally season the pork chops with salt and pepper. Push the celery-shallot mixture to the side of the skillet and add the pork chops. Raise the heat to high and brown them, about 1 minute per side.

4. Add the reduced white wine and bring to a boil. Lower the heat to medium, cover, and simmer for 5 to 6 minutes per side.

5. Transfer the pork chops to a serving platter and cover to keep warm. Add the dessert wine to the skillet and bring to a boil, scraping all the browned bits at the bottom of the pan. Return to the skillet any juices that the pork chops may have released, and season to taste with salt and pepper.

6. Top the pork chops with the wine sauce, sprinkle with the chopped celery leaves, and serve.

SEARED STEAK
WITH FIG GLAZE

Serves 4

According to Archestratus, the fourth-century B.C. gourmet, steak is best right "off the spit while it is still a bit on the rare side." Whether you enjoy your steak rare or well done, you'll love this fig glaze, which adds just the right amount of sweetness to the fiery peppercorn crust.

3 tablespoons whole five-color peppercorns, plus more to taste

Sirloin steak, about $2\frac{1}{2}$ pounds

Salt

2 tablespoons extra virgin olive oil

$\frac{3}{4}$ cup plus 1 tablespoon beef stock

6 whole dried figs, quartered

$\frac{1}{4}$ cup best-quality fruit vinegar

$\frac{1}{2}$ teaspoon all-purpose flour

1   Using the bottom of a heavy pan, coarsely crush the peppercorns in a sturdy plastic bag on a flat surface. Season the steak on both sides with a generous amount of salt and crushed peppercorns.

2   Heat the oil in a heavy skillet over very high heat. Sear the steak on both sides until firm to the touch, about 5 minutes per side for medium. Remove the steak and cover to keep warm.

3   Lower the heat to medium. Stir in ¾ cup of the stock and the figs, and scrape the pan to release all the browned bits of meat. Cook for 4 to 5 minutes, until the liquid is reduced by half and the figs are soft. Stir in the vinegar and boil gently for 2 to 3 minutes. Mix the flour with 1 tablespoon of the stock (or with water) until dissolved. Add to the sauce and stir to thicken. Season to taste with salt and crushed pepper. Place the steak on a platter and top with the sauce.

ORIGINAL RECIPE

Grind pepper which has been soaked overnight; add some more stock and work it into a smooth paste; thereupon add quince-apple cider, boiled down to half, that is which has evaporated in the heat of the sun to the consistency of honey. If this is not at hand, add dried fig concentrate that the Romans call "color." Now thicken the gravy with flour and water or with water in which rice has been boiled, and finish it on a gentle fire.

— ON COOKERY, APICIUS

⌘

MARCUS CICERO, the first-century B.C. Roman orator and statesman, studied philosophy in both Rome and Greece. At the end of his political career Cicero dedicated himself entirely to writing philosophy. Greatly influenced by the Epicureans, he agreed with their goal of achieving happiness through living life well and taking control of one's destiny. Cicero maintained that "the way to keep healthy is to know one's own constitution, to understand what is good for it and what is bad and to exercise moderation regarding all one's physical needs."

An avid letter writer, we learn Cicero's opinions on everything from politics to poetry in his correspondence. About friendship he wrote, "I entreat you to regard friendship as the finest thing in the world."

SAVORY PORK-FILLED ACORN SQUASH

Serves 4

Some men live to eat and drink, I eat and drink to live.

—SOCRATES, 470—399 B.C.

Socrates was legendary for his moderation, advising those who complained about a tasteless meal to "stop overeating, and you will then find life pleasanter, cheaper, and healthier." According to his friend the writer Xenophon, "Socrates ate just sufficient food to make eating a pleasure. . . . He found appetite the best seasoning." This dish is so delicious, it might have tempted even Socrates to overindulge a little. The succulent pork is a perfect match for squash and is great served alone or as a side dish for roast chicken or turkey.

2 acorn squash, about 1 pound each, halved and seeded

$\frac{1}{4}$ cup extra virgin olive oil

Salt and freshly milled pepper

1 medium onion, chopped

1 pound sweet pork sausage, crumbled

$\frac{1}{2}$ teaspoon anise seeds

$\frac{1}{4}$ teaspoon fennel seeds

8 ounces country-style bread, cubed

1 cup white wine

$\frac{1}{2}$ cup chicken stock

$\frac{1}{2}$ teaspoon ground cumin

$\frac{1}{4}$ cup coarsely chopped fresh parsley

1 cup shredded radicchio

1   Preheat the oven to 425° F.

2   Rub the squash halves with 2 tablespoons of oil and season generously with salt and pepper. Place, cut side down, on a lightly greased baking sheet and bake for 15 minutes.

3   Meanwhile, prepare the filling. Sauté the onion in the remaining 2 tablespoons of oil in a large nonstick skillet over medium-high heat until softened, about 5 minutes. Add the sausage, anise seeds, and fennel seeds, and cook until well browned, about 10 minutes. Transfer to a large bowl and mix with the bread cubes.

4 Add the wine, stock, cumin, and parsley to the skillet, stirring with a wooden spoon to loosen any browned bits. Bring the liquid to a simmer and cook until reduced by half, 5 to 6 minutes. Pour the liquid over the sausage-bread mixture and toss until absorbed. Season to taste with salt and pepper.

5 Lower the oven to 375° F. Divide the filling among the squash halves. Return the filled squash to the oven and bake for 15 to 20 minutes, or until the filling is browned and the squash is cooked through.

6 Serve topped with the shredded radicchio.

ORIGINAL RECIPE

Sweet fricassee of pumpkin. Put in the saucepan oil, liquamen [fermented fish sauce], stock, coriander, shoulder of pork cooked previously, and tiny meatballs. While this is cooking pound pepper, cumin, coriander—fresh or seed— fresh rue, asafetida root; moisten with vinegar, reduced wine, and some of the cooking liquid; blend with vinegar; bring to a boil. When it is boiling put in the saucepan pumpkin cleaned inside and out, diced, and boiled. Crumble pastry, and bind with this. Sprinkle with pepper and serve.

— ON COOKERY, APICIUS

WHEN SOCRATES was asked why he chose such a shrewish wife he answered, "I observe that men who wish to become expert horsemen do not get the most docile horses . . . so I have her, well assured that if I can endure her, I shall have no difficulty in my relations with the rest of humanity."

Even five hundred years after Socrates' death, historians were still fascinated with his wife Xanthippe's infamous "ill-tempered and quarrelsome" disposition. In Gellius's *Attic Nights*, a series of short essays on a variety of topics, one chapter was entitled "The witty reply of Socrates to his wife, Xanthippe, when she asked that they might spend more money for their dinners during the Dionysus festival." Sadly, not only is the entire chapter now lost, but the witty reply, too.

PORK LOIN WITH APPLES AND PANCETTA

Serves 6

Pork and apples have been paired since antiquity. This ancient Roman recipe, originally named after Gaius Matius, a writer and friend of Julius Caesar, combines leeks and tart green apples to create a moist and flavorful stuffing for pork loin. This is a great dish for a dinner party or buffet because it can be assembled ahead and baked just before guests arrive.

2 green apples, cored and diced

2 leeks, white and tender green parts, thinly sliced

3 tablespoons olive oil

$\frac{1}{4}$ cup cider or other fruit vinegar

1 tablespoon honey

$\frac{1}{2}$ teaspoon ground cumin

$\frac{1}{2}$ teaspoon ground coriander

Salt and freshly milled pepper

1 pork loin roast, butterflied, about 4 pounds deboned

12 thin slices pancetta, about 4 ounces

1 Sauté the apples and leeks in the oil in a small skillet over high heat until softened, about 3 minutes. Add the vinegar, honey, cumin, and coriander, and simmer until the vinegar has evaporated. Season to taste with salt and pepper. Allow the mixture to cool slightly.

2 Preheat the oven to 450° F.

3 Spread the mixture in the center of the pork loin, roll to close, and tie with kitchen string. Liberally season the outside of the pork loin with salt and pepper. Wrap the pancetta slices very snuggly around the pork loin, slightly overlapping them. Roast in a baking pan for 10 minutes and then lower the heat to 325° F. Cook for about 25 minutes per pound.

⌐⌐

IN HIS PLAY *Birds*, Aristophanes joked, "These impossible women! How they do get around us! The poet was right: can't live with them, or without them." In ancient Greece, while men may have lived with women, they certainly didn't dine with them. Women were present at feasts only to serve the men, but they ate later. Even in poor households the women and children ate after the men because it was thought that since they required less food, they should eat the men's leftovers.

GINGERSNAP-CRUSTED PORK LOIN WITH BRANDIED FIG SAUCE

Serves 4

In ancient Rome, the skin of fresh ham was scored in diamond shapes and the ham was baked in honey, just as we do today. For variety the Romans sometimes coated the ham with figs and spiced bread crumbs, the inspiration for this modern recipe.

Crushed gingersnap cookies make a tasty coating that also keeps the meat tender and moist. You may also want to try this delicious brandied fig sauce with cheese, prosciutto, or salami.

1 pork tenderloin, about 1 pound

Salt and freshly milled pepper

2 tablespoons honey

$\frac{1}{2}$ cup crushed gingersnap cookies

$\frac{1}{2}$ cup sliced dried figs

$1\frac{1}{4}$ cups brandy

$\frac{3}{4}$ cup chicken stock, plus more as needed

$\frac{1}{4}$ teaspoon dry mustard

1 Preheat the oven to 425° F.

2 Liberally season the pork loin with salt and pepper. Drizzle 1 tablespoon of the honey over the entire loin and press on the gingersnap crumbs. Place the pork loin on a rack in a roasting pan and cook for 18 to 22 minutes per pound or until a meat thermometer reads 160° to 170° F.

3 Meanwhile, bring the figs and brandy to a boil in a small saucepan over medium-high heat. Add the stock, the mustard, and the remaining 1 tablespoon of honey. Simmer for 10 minutes, until the figs are soft. Once the mixture cools, puree it in a food processor. If it is too thick, add a bit more stock. Season to taste with salt and pepper, and set aside.

4 Remove the pork loin from the oven and allow it to rest for 5 minutes before slicing. Serve the slices topped with a dollop of brandied fig sauce.

LAMB WITH POMEGRANATE-GLAZED ONIONS

Serves 4

Graffiti uncovered on the wall of a restaurant in Pompeii read, *"Ubi perna cocta est si convivae apponitur non gusat pernam linguit ollam aut caccabum,"* or roughly translated, "The guests lick the pans here." This dish, based on a Roman recipe and as tantalizing to the eye as to the palate, just might get your guests licking the pans, too.

The slightly tart pomegranate mixes wonderfully with the sweet caramelized onions to provide a perfect backdrop to the lamb. This is a great dish to serve when you have company because it needs a minimum of attention but delivers gourmet results.

1 tablespoon ground cumin

1 tablespoon cumin seeds

1 tablespoon dried thyme

1 teaspoon dried savory

1 tablespoon ground coriander

1 tablespoon coarsely crushed coriander seeds

1 boneless leg of lamb, about $2\frac{1}{2}$ pounds

Salt and freshly milled pepper

1 pound assorted red, yellow, and white pearl onions

1 teaspoon brown sugar

$\frac{1}{4}$ cup raspberry or fruit vinegar

$\frac{1}{2}$ cup pomegranate seeds

1　Combine the ground cumin, cumin seeds, thyme, savory, ground coriander, and crushed coriander seeds in a small bowl. Press the spice mixture on all sides of the lamb. Cover with plastic wrap and refrigerate for at least 2 hours or overnight.

2　Preheat the oven to 350° F. Liberally season the spice-crusted lamb with salt and pepper. Place the lamb, fat side up, on a rack in a roasting pan on the middle shelf of the oven. Lower the heat to 325° F and bake for 28 to 30 minutes per pound, or until a meat thermometer reads 150° F for rare. Add the onions to the pan for the final 30 minutes.

3　Remove the meat from the roasting pan and allow to rest for 10 minutes before carving. While the meat is resting, place the roasting pan with the onions on a stovetop burner over high heat. Sprinkle the onions with the brown sugar, the vinegar, and 3 tablespoons of the pomegranate seeds. Cook until the vinegar is reduced by half, about 2 minutes. Season to taste with salt and pepper.

4 Slice the lamb and arrange it on a serving platter surrounded by the glazed onions. Garnish with the remaining 5 tablespoons pomegranate seeds.

ORIGINAL RECIPE

Epaenetus in his *Art of Cookery* gives this recipe: A myma [meaning unknown to modern translators] of any kind of meat, including fowl, should be made by cutting up the tender parts of the meat into small pieces, mashing in the liver, intestines, and blood, and spicing with vinegar, melted cheese, silphium, cumin, fresh and dried thyme, savory, fresh and dried coriander, geteion [meaning unknown to modern translators], common peeled onions roasted, or poppy seeds, raisins, or honey or the pips of an acid pomegranate.

—*THE PHILOSOPHER'S BANQUET*, ATHENAEUS

IT WAS considered the height of poor manners to discuss business or even ask why a stranger had arrived at your door until he was offered food and refreshments. In the *Odyssey*, for example, when Odysseus suddenly appeared at the hut of a poor swineherd, the man, although curious, politely said, "When you have had all the bread and wine you want, you shall tell me where you come from and what your troubles are."

VEAL CHOPS WITH QUINCE AND LEEKS

Serves 2

Time is flying, never to return.
—VIRGIL, 70–19 B.C.

When asked what was the proper time for dinner, Diogenes, the fourth-century B.C. Greek philosopher, sagely replied, "If you are a rich man, whenever you please; and if you are a poor man, whenever you can."

In antiquity, just as today, guests were invited to dinner at a specific time, and arriving late was considered rude. Punctuality was a frequent theme in poems and plays. The fourth-century B.C. Greek poet Amphis went so far as to say that a man who arrives late for a dinner invitation is probably the first who will desert his fellow soldiers in the battlefield.

1 leek, white and tender green parts, thinly sliced

1 quince or green apple, peeled, quartered, cored, and sliced

$\frac{1}{2}$ teaspoon ground thyme

$\frac{1}{2}$ teaspoon dried oregano

$\frac{1}{4}$ cup olive oil

Salt and freshly milled pepper

4 rib veal chops, about 8 ounces each

1 cup white wine

$\frac{1}{4}$ cup veal or chicken stock

1   Sauté the leek, quince, thyme, and oregano in 2 tablespoons of the oil in a large nonstick skillet over medium heat until softened, 6 to 7 minutes. Season to taste with salt and pepper, remove from the skillet, and set aside.

2   Add the remaining 2 tablespoons of oil and the chops to the skillet. Sear on both sides over high heat until cooked through, 3 to 4 minutes per side. Remove and keep warm.

3   Pour in the wine, scraping up any browned bits, and return the quince-leek mixture to the pan. Add the stock and simmer at a low boil until the liquid is reduced by half, about 3 minutes.

4   Pour the warm quince-leek sauce over the chops and serve.

ORIGINAL RECIPE

Veal or beef with leeks or quinces or onions, or with dasheens [taro]. Liquamen [fermented fish sauce], pepper, asafetida, and a little oil.

— *ON COOKERY*, APICIUS

MARINATED BEEF TENDERLOIN WITH CUCUMBER-ONION RELISH

Serves 6

Recipe after recipe in Apicius's Roman cookbook reads as only a list of ingredients without any of the usual commentary and detail we are used to in contemporary cookbooks. When I came across this recipe that ended with the promise "You will be amazed," my attention was piqued, and I had to try it.

The result is a dry marinade of pickling spices for tenderloin served with a delicious creamy relish. As promised in the two-thousand-year-old recipe, you and your guests will indeed be amazed.

2 heaping tablespoons prepackaged pickling spices (If you prefer to make this yourself, use $\frac{1}{8}$ teaspoon ground cinnamon, $1\frac{1}{2}$ teaspoons whole allspice berries, $\frac{1}{4}$ teaspoon yellow mustard seeds, 1 teaspoon coriander seeds, 2 bay leaves, 1 teaspoon red pepper flakes, 10 whole cloves, and $\frac{1}{8}$ teaspoon freshly milled black pepper.)

One $1\frac{1}{2}$-pound beef tenderloin

Salt

$\frac{1}{2}$ European cucumber, finely diced, about 1 cup

2 teaspoons sugar

1 small red onion, finely minced

3 red radishes, finely minced

$\frac{1}{4}$ cup minced fresh mint

1 tablespoon freshly squeezed lemon juice

$\frac{1}{4}$ cup Greek-style yogurt, drained yogurt, or sour cream

1 Grind the pickling spices in a clean coffee grinder or mortar. Firmly press the spices on all sides of the tenderloin. Cover with plastic wrap and refrigerate for 2 hours or overnight so the spices can flavor the meat.

2 Preheat the oven to 375° F. Liberally salt the tenderloin, place it on a rack in a roasting pan, and bake for about 18 minutes per pound for medium. Allow to rest for 5 minutes before slicing.

3 Meanwhile, prepare the relish. Mix the cucumber, sugar, and ½ teaspoon of salt in a small bowl and allow to stand for 10 minutes. Drain the liquid that forms. Stir in the onion, radishes, mint, lemon juice, and yogurt.

4 Serve the sliced tenderloin with the relish on the side.

AFTER dinner the Greeks regularly gathered to drink and discuss philosophy at wine parties called symposia.

Wine, more potent then, was diluted and frequently cooled with snow that was carried down from mountaintops wrapped in insulating wool or straw. The host of a symposium determined the ratio of water to wine and even the size of the wine goblets, depending on how intoxicated he wanted his guests. Aristophanes, the fourth-century B.C. playwright, joked, "When men drink, then they are rich and successful and win lawsuits, and are happy and help their friends. Quickly, bring me a beaker of wine, so that I may wet my mind and say something clever."

SEASONED SALT

Makes about $\frac{1}{2}$ cup

Once it had burned down and the flames died away, he scattered the coals and, stretching the spitted meat across the embers, raised them onto supports and sprinkled them with divine salts.

—HOMER, CIRCA 700 B.C.

Salt, always used in sacrifices to the gods, was considered a gift of nature, a connection between man and the heavens. Homer called it "divine," and Plato referred to it as "a substance dear to the gods." The ancient Greeks and Romans considered it bad luck to spill salt or leave a saltshaker on the table after a meal.

The original recipe claimed that this salt mix was "good for the digestion . . . and for averting all sorts of sicknesses and plagues and chills." I'm not certain of its health benefits, but this irresistible blend of seasonings sprinkled on just before grilling or roasting adds a distinctive and unusual flavor to meat, poultry, fish, and vegetables. I make large batches and put the salt in decorative jars to give as gifts.

2 bay leaves
$\frac{1}{2}$ cup coarse sea salt
1 tablespoon dried rosemary
$1\frac{1}{2}$ teaspoons dried mint
$1\frac{1}{2}$ teaspoons dried parsley
$1\frac{1}{2}$ teaspoons dried thyme
1 teaspoon anise seeds
1 teaspoon celery seeds
$\frac{1}{2}$ teaspoon freshly milled pepper
$\frac{1}{2}$ teaspoon dried oregano or marjoram
$\frac{1}{4}$ teaspoon ground cumin

1 Place the bay leaves on the bottom of an airtight jar. Add the salt, rosemary, mint, parsley, thyme, anise seeds, celery seeds, pepper, oregano, and cumin to the jar. Close the jar and shake to mix the ingredients.

2 Liberally sprinkle on any meats, fish, or vegetables just before cooking. Store the unused salt in a cool, dry place.

THE ATHENIANS, considered the master bakers of classical times, created breads flavored with honey, olives, cumin, garlic, coriander, fennel, capers, or sage. The ancients even baked with rice flour, describing rice as "a seed grown in Ethiopia and resembles sesame."

Similar to today, bread was made with milk, water, wine, or oil and shaped into crescents, animals, fruits, or vegetables. Some bread was even shaped to resemble male genitalia, but with practical rather than lewd connotations, celebrating the intimate connection between food and sex, production and reproduction.

Chapter 7

PANIS: BREADS

POPPY SEED BREAD OF ATHENS

CRISP CHICKPEA WEDGES

CHEESE BISCUITS WITH AROMATIC BAY LEAVES

PEPPER TWISTS

BARLEY ROLLS OF LESBOS

QUINCE AND GINGER MUFFINS

HERB CRISPS

ETRUSCAN FOCACCIA

CHEESE AND ANISE SEED QUICK BREAD

HONEY-FETA GRIDDLE BREAD

POPPY SEED BREAD OF ATHENS

Makes 1 loaf

Very fine, too, is the wheat loaf made for the market,
which glorious Athens supplies to mortals.

—ARCHESTRATUS, CIRCA FOURTH CENTURY B.C.

This recipe from *The Philosopher's Banquet* was written in the first century A.D. The book mentions more than seventy kinds of bread baked by the Greeks, Romans, and Egyptians. This wonderfully tasty bread was originally baked in a round pan so that it would form a mushroom shape. Whether you bake it in a round, square, or rectangular pan, you'll thoroughly enjoy this honey-and-poppy-seed-flavored treat.

1 package active dry yeast

$\frac{1}{2}$ cup warm whole milk

2 tablespoons honey

$2\frac{1}{2}$ cups all-purpose flour, plus more as needed

2 teaspoons salt

2 tablespoons olive oil, plus more for greasing the bowl

$\frac{1}{2}$ cup whole wheat flour

2 tablespoons poppy seeds

1   Mix the yeast, milk, and honey in a small bowl and allow to rest until the yeast dissolves and begins to foam, about 10 minutes. Combine the flour and salt in a large bowl. Slowly stir in the milk mixture, $\frac{1}{2}$ cup of warm water, and the oil. Beat for 2 minutes with an electric mixer set on medium speed. Scrape down the sides of the bowl, add the whole wheat flour, and beat until the dough forms a ball.

2   Lightly flour a work surface. Knead the dough until smooth and elastic, about 10 minutes. Add flour as necessary to keep the dough from sticking to the surface.

3   Grease a large bowl with oil, sprinkle with the poppy seeds, and turn the dough several times in the bowl. Cover and put in a warm place to rise, about 1 hour.

4   Punch the dough down on a floured work surface and place it in a lightly oiled 6- to 7-inch round bread pan. Cover and allow to rise again for about 1 hour.

5   Preheat the oven to 400° F.

6   Bake until golden brown, about 30 minutes. Allow to cool on a rack before slicing.

ORIGINAL RECIPE

There is also a "boletus" bread, so-called, shaped like a mushroom. The kneading bowl is greased and sprinkled with poppy seed, on which the dough is spread, and so it does not stick during rising. When it is placed in the oven, some coarse meal is sprinkled over the earthenware pan, after which the loaf is laid upon it and takes on a delightful color, like that of smoked cheese.

—*THE PHILOSOPHER'S BANQUET,* ATHENAEUS

CRISP CHICKPEA WEDGES
Serves 6

Galen, the second-century physician whose writings influenced medicine throughout the Renaissance, describes various recipes for chickpeas, including these crisp baked wedges that make a perfect side dish to any meal. They are also great as appetizers served with olives, cheeses, or salamis. Chickpeas were thought to be an aphrodisiac. Perhaps it is that belief or just their wonderful taste that accounts for the many chickpea recipes still found throughout the Mediterranean area today, such as Sicilian *panelle* and Greek *pitaroudia*.

$3/4$ cup chickpea flour

$1\frac{1}{2}$ cups vegetable or chicken stock

$\frac{1}{2}$ teaspoon salt

$\frac{1}{4}$ teaspoon freshly milled pepper

2 tablespoons minced fresh parsley

2 garlic cloves, minced

3 tablespoons extra virgin olive oil

$\frac{1}{2}$ teaspoon dried oregano

$\frac{1}{4}$ cup grated Parmesan cheese

1   Whisk the chickpea flour, stock, salt, pepper, parsley, and garlic in a bowl until smooth. Cover the bowl with plastic wrap and refrigerate for 1 hour to allow the flavors to mingle.

2   Place a rack in the lowest position of the oven and preheat the oven to 500° F.

3   Trim a piece of parchment to fit in the bottom of a 9-inch round cake pan and brush with 1 tablespoon of the oil. Add the remaining 2 tablespoons of oil, the oregano, and the cheese to the chickpea mixture and stir. Pour the mixture into the cake pan and smooth the surface evenly with a spatula or spoon.

4   Bake until dry and golden, 15 to 20 minutes. Slice into wedges and serve hot.

AESOP, thought to have been a Greek slave, left us such enduring fables as "The Wolf in Sheep's Clothing," "The Lion and the Mouse," "The Fox and the Grapes," "The Hare and the Tortoise," and "The Goose and the Golden Eggs."

Gellius, the second-century historian, wrote of Aesop, "By inventing witty entertaining fables he put into men's minds and hearts ideas that were wholesome and carefully considered." Gellius recounted a fable attributed to Aesop about a wise mother lark whose nest was situated in a field of wheat ready for harvest. She warned her chicks that when the field was to be cut, they would have to leave quickly because their nest would be exposed. However, to the chicks' surprise, the mother lark did not budge when she heard the farmer arranging for help from his friends, neighbors, and relatives. Only days later when no help arrived and she overheard the farmer say that he was going to do the work himself did the mother lark quickly gather her chicks and leave. Aesop's moral: We can only count on ourselves to get a job done.

CHEESE BISCUITS WITH AROMATIC BAY LEAVES

Makes 1 dozen biscuits

Let us recall Marcus Cato the Censor,
who first taught Agriculture to speak Latin.

—COLUMELLA, FIRST CENTURY A.D.

Cato's book, *On Agriculture*, dating from the second century B.C., is the earliest surviving complete work in Latin prose. In it Cato comments that sharing a meal helps create bonds between people, and he calls the dinner table "highly friend-making."

Besides recipes, Cato gives lots of practical advice, including where to buy togas and shoes (in Rome) and oil (in Pompeii); he also explains how to make natural pesticides and suggests the best spot to build a kitchen and wine cellar.

Serve these light, flaky biscuits to guests for your own "friend-making."

$3/_4$ cup all-purpose flour

$1/_2$ teaspoon baking powder

$1/_2$ teaspoon salt

$1/_2$ teaspoon freshly milled pepper

1 cup whole-milk ricotta cheese

1 large egg

2 tablespoons grated Parmesan cheese

1 dried bay leaf, crumbled

1 Preheat the oven to 375° F. Grease a baking sheet and set aside.

2 Stir together the flour, baking powder, salt, and pepper in a large bowl. Stir the ricotta and the egg into the flour mixture until well combined. Drop by rounded tablespoonfuls onto the baking sheet. Top each biscuit with the grated Parmesan and a few flakes of the crumbled bay leaf.

3 Bake until golden, 15 to 20 minutes. Serve warm.

ORIGINAL RECIPE

Recipe for libum [cake for religious offerings]: Bray 2 pounds of cheese thoroughly in a mortar; when it is thoroughly macerated, add 1 pound of wheat flour, or, if you wish the cake to be more dainty, $\frac{1}{2}$ pound of fine flour, and mix thoroughly with the cheese. Add 1 egg, and work the whole well. Pat out a loaf, place on bay leaves, and bake slowly on a warm hearth under a crock.

—*ON AGRICULTURE*, CATO THE ELDER

PLATO did not begin writing about philosophy until after the death of his teacher, Socrates. Plato wrote on a wide variety of topics, including food and drink. He thought it beneficial for men to gather together to drink and discuss life, and he advocated initiating boys to alcohol at a young age to avoid drunkenness and excess later. While he endorsed drinking wine, he was suspicious of fancy foods and chefs, calling cookery the "art of deception."

In his dialogue, *The Republic*, Plato describes a simple dinner in an ideal world: "For food they will make meal from their barley, and flour from their wheat, and kneading and baking them they will heap their noble scones and loaves on reeds or fresh leaves, and lying on couches, they will have salt and olives and cheese, and they will have boiled dishes with onions and such vegetables as one gets in the country. And I expect we must allow them a dessert of figs, and peas and beans, and they will roast myrtle berries and acorns at the fire, and drink their wine in moderation."

PEPPER TWISTS

Makes 1 dozen twists

According to Greek myth, a mortal once helped Demeter, the goddess of harvest. As a reward, Demeter taught him how to plant and harvest wheat and gave him seeds, a wooden plow, and a chariot drawn by serpents to travel the world and teach the rest of mankind the art of agriculture.

These bread twists certainly seem like a gift from the gods. Their classic combination of honey, wine, and pepper make them a perfect appetizer or dinner bread. I like to dip them in honey that has been simmered with herbs.

$1\frac{1}{2}$ cups white wine

1 package active dry yeast

$1\frac{1}{2}$ tablespoons whole five-color peppercorns

2 teaspoons salt

2 tablespoons unsalted butter, softened

$1\frac{3}{4}$ cups all-purpose flour, plus more as needed

2 large eggs

2 tablespoons sugar

$\frac{1}{2}$ cup whole wheat flour

1   Bring the wine to a slow boil in a small saucepan and simmer until reduced to $\frac{3}{4}$ cup. Transfer the wine to a medium bowl and allow to cool to room temperature. Add the yeast and stir to dissolve.

2   On a work surface, crush the peppercorns in a sturdy plastic bag or under a kitchen towel with the back of a skillet until coarsely ground. Add 1 tablespoon of the crushed pepper, the salt, the butter, and 1 cup of the all-purpose flour to the yeast mixture. Using an electric beater set on medium, blend for 2 minutes.

3   Add 1 egg, the sugar, and the whole wheat flour, and continue beating. Add the remaining $\frac{3}{4}$ cup of all-purpose flour, a little at a time, until the dough is firm and workable. Turn the dough out onto a lightly floured surface and knead for about 5 minutes. Set aside in a lightly greased bowl, covered, and allow to settle for 30 minutes.

4   On a lightly floured surface, take small handfuls of the dough and roll into 5-inch-long strips about $\frac{1}{2}$ inch wide. Take 2 strips and gently twist them together, pinching the ends to seal and prevent unraveling.

5   Place the twists on a lightly greased baking sheet and allow to rise for about 30 minutes.

6   Preheat the oven to 375° F.

7   Beat the remaining egg well and, using a pastry brush, coat the tops and sides of the twists. Sprinkle the remaining crushed pepper on top and place the twists in the oven. Bake for about 15 minutes, or until golden and cooked through. Serve warm.

ORIGINAL RECIPE

Twist bread is prepared with the mixture of a little milk; there is added also a little pepper and oil or lard.

—*THE PHILOSOPHER'S BANQUET*, ATHENAEUS

Pepper Twists (left)
and Herb Crisps (right)

BARLEY ROLLS OF LESBOS

Makes 13 rolls

The stars about the lovely moon hide their shining forms
when it lights up the earth at its fullest.

—SAPPHO, CIRCA 610—580 B.C.

The Sicilian-Greek fourth-century B.C. gourmet Archestratus praises the honey-sweetened barley bread of the island of Lesbos, home of the poet Sappho. So esteemed was the baking of Lesbos that according to legend the messenger god Hermes got bread there for all the other gods.

These honey-sweet, easy-to-make rolls are heavenly with dinner, and if any are left over, they reheat nicely for breakfast.

1 package active dry yeast

1 cup warm whole milk

$\frac{1}{3}$ cup honey

1 teaspoon salt

2 tablespoons olive oil, plus more as needed

2 large eggs

1 cup barley flour

2 cups all-purpose flour

1 Combine the yeast, milk, honey, salt, oil, and 1 egg in the bowl of an electric mixer. Beat on low speed until combined, about 1 minute. Slowly add the barley and all-purpose flours, and continue to beat for another minute. Increase the speed to medium and mix until the dough forms a ball.

2 Place the dough in a lightly oiled bowl and turn it once to coat all sides with oil. Cover with plastic wrap and allow to rise in a draft-free spot at room temperature for about 1 hour.

3 Pull off small pieces of the dough and knead to form balls that are about $1\frac{1}{2}$ inches in diameter; you should get about 13. Place the balls, just touching, in a well-greased 9-inch round baking pan. Pierce the top of each roll a few times with a sharp knife. Beat the remaining egg well and, using a pastry brush, coat the tops of the rolls. Loosely cover with plastic wrap. Allow the pan of rolls to rise in a warm spot until doubled in size, about 1 hour.

4 Preheat the oven to 350° F.

5 Remove the plastic wrap, place the pan in the oven, and bake for about 40 minutes, or until golden. Serve warm.

HOMER, the eighth-century B.C. epic poet, mentions bread throughout his works, calling it the "marrow of man's bones."

In the *Iliad* he poetically describes the plowing of a field of wheat: "Across it crews of plowmen wheeled their teams, driving them up and back and soon as they'd reach the end-strip, moving into the turn, a man would run up quickly and hand them a cup of honeyed, mellow wine, as the crews would then back down along the furrows, pressing again to reach the end of the deep fallow field and the earth churned black behind them, like earth churning."

QUINCE AND GINGER MUFFINS

Makes 1 dozen muffins

Quinces have a wonderful fragrance and firm flesh, and were often used in ancient cooking. Try these marvelous muffins for breakfast or as an accompaniment to roast chicken or pork. They are also terrific made with tart green apple.

$1\frac{3}{4}$ cups all-purpose flour

$\frac{1}{4}$ cup brown sugar

2 teaspoons baking powder

2 tablespoons grated fresh ginger

$\frac{1}{2}$ teaspoon ground nutmeg

$\frac{1}{2}$ teaspoon salt

$\frac{1}{4}$ teaspoon ground white pepper

$\frac{1}{4}$ cup honey

1 large egg

$\frac{1}{4}$ cup almond or walnut oil

$\frac{1}{2}$ cup frozen apple juice concentrate, thawed

1 quince or green apple, peeled, cored, and grated

1   Preheat the oven to 400° F. Lightly grease a 12-cup muffin pan.

2   Combine the flour, brown sugar, baking powder, ginger, nutmeg, salt, and pepper in a large bowl. In a separate bowl, mix the honey, egg, oil, and apple juice. Add to the dry ingredients and mix with an electric beater set on low until just combined. Stir in the quince.

3   Divide the batter evenly among the muffin cups. Bake in the center of the oven until golden and a toothpick inserted in the center comes out clean, 20 to 23 minutes.

ORIGINAL RECIPE

In Syria is made a quince-cake, which lasts for such a long time that containers packed with it are exported to Rome. It is made from honey and the flesh of quinces that has been pulped and boiled with honey.

My medicine, which I make for those suffering from a loss of appetite, is made not only from honey and apple juice, but also contains a little white pepper, ginger, and vinegar.

—*ON THE POWERS OF FOODS*, BOOK 2, GALEN

HERB CRISPS

Makes 4 dozen

A crust eaten in peace is better than
feasting at a banquet in anxiety.
—AESOP, CIRCA 500 B.C.

In the original two-thousand-year-old recipe, the herb-dough strips were fried, but these were baked for a lighter taste and easier preparation. This delicious treat is wonderful for dipping and takes less than twenty minutes to prepare, including the baking time. It is perfect for unexpected guests or when you feel like having homemade bread but don't want to wait. Photograph on page 181.

1 large egg, lightly beaten

2 tablespoons white wine

1 tablespoon olive oil, plus more for greasing the baking sheet

1 tablespoon honey

1 cup all-purpose flour, plus more for flouring the work surface

1 teaspoon salt

$\frac{1}{4}$ cup minced assorted fresh herbs, such as parsley, basil, and rosemary, or $1\frac{1}{2}$ tablespoons assorted dried herbs

1   Preheat the oven to 475° F.

2   Combine the egg, wine, oil, honey, flour, salt, and herbs in a small bowl. Mix with a fork and then knead to finish combining the ingredients.

3   Divide the dough in half. Shape each half into a long log about 2 inches in diameter. Lightly flour a work surface and roll out 1 log to a rectangular shape about 4 inches wide, 12 inches long, and ¼ inch thick. Using a sharp knife, cut into strips about 4 inches long and 1 inch wide. Repeat for the remaining log.

4   Lightly coat a nonstick baking sheet with oil and place the strips on the sheet. Bake for 5 to 6 minutes, or until golden. Serve warm.

ORIGINAL RECIPE

The catillus ornatus, as the Romans call it, is made in the following manner: Wash and scrape some lettuce, pour wine into a mortar and mash the strips of lettuce, and after squeezing off the juice, knead fine wheat flour into it; let it settle for a while, then mash it vigorously, adding a little pork fat and some pepper, and mashing it again, draw it out into a thin slab; smooth, trim, and cut it into pieces; then place the pieces in a strainer and boil them in very hot olive oil.

—"BREAD-MAKING," CHRYSIPPUS,
IN *THE PHILOSOPHER'S BANQUET*, ATHENAEUS

BOTH literary and art sources have shown that the Egyptians, who ran public bakeries as early as the twelfth century B.C., kneaded dough with their feet and taught this and other bread-making techniques to the Greeks.

ETRUSCAN FOCACCIA

Makes 2 loaves

*When a loaf of bread is in the oven, cracks appear in it here and there;
and these flaws, though not intended in the baking, have a
rightness of their own, and sharpen the appetite.*

—MARCUS AURELIUS, A.D. 121—180

The Etruscans settled on the west coast of central Italy in roughly the eighth century B.C. Although there are many surviving stone tablets with Etruscan writing, scholars have not yet been able to translate their language. We know from archaeological remains, however, that they made a kind of thick dough from ground grains. It was baked under hot cooking ashes and then topped with seasoned oils, herbs, and other available ingredients. The Romans called these ashcakes *panus focus*, which evolved into the Italian *focaccia*.

Modern focaccia is simple to make because the shape isn't important and the dough is very forgiving. In fact, as Marcus Aurelius noted in the above quote, the more rustic and irregular, the better. It is great bread for the little fingers in your family.

1 package active dry yeast

2 tablespoons honey

2 cups all-purpose flour, plus more as needed

5 tablespoons extra virgin olive oil

2 tablespoons salt

Semolina flour or cornmeal for dusting the pan

1 teaspoon dried rosemary

1 teaspoon dried marjoram

1 tablespoon coarse sea salt

1 Mix the yeast, honey, and 1 cup of warm water in a small bowl until the yeast dissolves.

2 In a large bowl, combine the all-purpose flour, 2 tablespoons of the oil, and the 2 tablespoons of salt. Slowly add the yeast mixture, a little at a time, combining with a fork or an electric mixer.

3 Lightly flour your hands and a work surface, and knead the dough, adding a bit more water or flour as necessary to keep it from sticking. Knead for about 5 minutes, until the

dough feels elastic. Place the dough in a lightly greased bowl, poke it a few times with a knife, and allow to rise, covered, in a warm, dry spot until it doubles in size, about 1 hour.

4 Knead the dough again for a few minutes, then divide in half. With the palm of your hand, press each half into a rectangle about 6 inches by 10 inches. Place the rectangles on a baking sheet liberally dusted with semolina flour.

5 Mix the rosemary and marjoram with 2 tablespoons of the oil in a small bowl and spread on the focaccia. Repeatedly press the herbs and the oil into the dough with your fingertips. Allow to rise for 30 to 40 minutes.

6 Preheat the oven to 500° F.

7 Bake until golden, about 15 minutes. Drizzle with the remaining tablespoon of oil and sprinkle with the tablespoon of coarse salt.

POMPEII, a resort town for wealthy Romans and an important port of trade, was buried by the eruption of Mount Vesuvius in A.D. 79. The resulting airtight covering of volcanic ash provided us with a frozen moment in time that offers a unique glimpse of the everyday life of ancient Rome.

Archaeologists learned a lot about Roman bread-making techniques by studying the wheat-grinding mills and the more than twenty bakeries unearthed in the ruins. Many types of bread were discovered, both on home tables and in these bakeries. As a testimony to the suddenness of the disaster, one bakery even had eighty-one loaves of bread still in its ovens.

CHEESE AND ANISE SEED QUICK BREAD

Serves 8

The breads of Greece are "like a magnet that draw the hungry to them," according to Eubulus, the fourth-century Greek poet. Described in *On Cookery* by Heracleides as "bread shaped like dice made with anise seed, cheese, and oil," this moist and aromatic delight, similar in texture to banana bread, is quick to make because it needs no kneading or time to rise.

$1\frac{1}{2}$ cups all-purpose flour

1 teaspoon salt

$1\frac{1}{2}$ teaspoons baking powder

1 teaspoon anise seeds

$\frac{1}{2}$ teaspoon ground cumin

$\frac{3}{4}$ cup cottage cheese

$\frac{3}{4}$ teaspoon olive oil

2 large eggs

1 tablespoon honey

1 Preheat the oven to 375° F. Lightly grease an 8 by 8-inch square baking pan and set aside.

2 Stir together the flour, salt, baking powder, anise seeds, and cumin in a bowl until combined. In another bowl, whisk together the cottage cheese, oil, eggs, and honey until combined. Add the dry ingredients and stir until just blended. Spread the dough evenly in the pan.

3 Bake until golden brown, 20 to 25 minutes. Cut into squares and serve warm.

The people that once bestowed commands, consulships,
legions, and all else, now concerns itself no more, and longs
eagerly for just two things—bread and circuses!
—DECIMUS JUNIUS JUVENAL, A.D. 55–127

JULIUS CAESAR publicized his military victories by hosting feasts and entertainments. To promote his triumphs in Egypt and Libya he organized a five-day celebration that included staged plays, gladiator fights, combat with wild beasts, and athletic contests and races. A historian of the time described the events in this way: "Young men of the highest rank drove four-horse and two-horse chariots . . . vaulting from one to the other," and the celebration concluded with "a battle between two opposing armies, in which five hundred foot-soldiers, twenty elephants, and thirty horsemen engaged on each side."

HONEY-FETA GRIDDLE BREAD

Serves 6

According to Greek myth, Apollo fathered a child with a mortal princess. Their son was taught both the arts of cheese-making and bee-keeping, which he then passed on to man. These gifts of cheese and honey combine in this recipe to create heavenly griddle bread.

This irresistible griddle bread is very versatile; it is delicious wrapped around cured meats or grilled asparagus, and when used to scoop up stews and dips.

4 ounces feta cheese

2 tablespoons honey

$\frac{1}{2}$ teaspoon salt

$\frac{1}{2}$ cup all-purpose flour, plus more as needed

1 In a large bowl, mash the cheese, honey, and salt together with a fork until well combined. Add the flour and mix until a dough forms. Turn the dough out onto a work surface and knead briefly. Cover with plastic wrap and allow to rest at room temperature for about 20 minutes.

2 Divide the dough into 12 equal pieces. Lightly flour a work surface and roll each piece into a very thin circle about 3 inches in diameter.

3 Lightly oil a nonstick griddle and heat over medium-low heat. Grill each circle until golden, about 1 minute per side. Oil the griddle after each use.

4 Serve warm.

ORIGINAL RECIPE

Now the phthois is made in the following manner: Squeeze off a piece of cheese, mash it, put it in a bronze sieve and strain it through, then pour on honey and a cup of finest wheat flour and work it into a soft lump.

—"BREAD-MAKING," CHRYSIPPUS,
IN *THE PHILOSOPHER'S BANQUET*, ATHENAEUS

If you want to try a dessert, I can offer you raisins (my own), pears (from Syria), and hot chestnuts (grown in Naples, city of learning), roasted in a slow-burning fire.

—MARTIAL, A.D. 40–103

AS MARTIAL, the first-century poet, illustrates, the ancients often ended a meal with nuts and fresh fruit.

Fruit, prized for its natural sweetness, inspired many myths and fables, such as one about an apple and a peach bickering about who was more delicious until a blackberry from a nearby bush intervened, reminding them that there was really no point in arguing, since they were part of the same family anyway.

In another Aesop fable, an avaricious landlord, not satisfied with receiving all the fruit from an apple tree growing on land he leased to others, uprooted it. No sooner had the tree been removed than it withered and died. Aesop's moral: Greed harms.

Chapter 8

AMBROSIA: DESSERTS

DATES IN SPICED WINE

MEDITERRANEAN FRUIT SALAD

PEACHES IN SPICED WINE

HAZEL-WALNUT HONEY CUSTARD

BAY LEAF COOKIES

CANDY NUT CHEWS

MILK AND HONEY DESSERT TOASTS

FIG GRANITA

WALNUT CAKE WITH FIG JAM

PHYLLO-WRAPPED ALMOND SEMOLINA

LAVENDER-HONEY APPLES IN PUFF PASTRY

MINI RICOTTA FRITTERS

DATES IN SPICED WINE

Serves 4

Nothing can nourish the human body
unless it participates in some sweetness.

—ARISTOTLE, 384—322 B.C.

Sugar, believed to have medicinal benefits, was prescribed as a cure for everything from headaches to melancholy. Foods naturally sweet such as dates and honey were highly prized, and many ancient recipes combined the two. Simple to prepare, these stuffed dates offer a unique combination of sweet and spicy so reminiscent of antiquity. Serve them with a wedge of your favorite cheese for another classic taste pairing.

12 large dates

3 tablespoons coarsely chopped blanched almonds

2 tablespoons coarsely chopped walnuts

$\frac{1}{2}$ cup red wine

2 tablespoons honey

$\frac{1}{2}$ teaspoon freshly milled five-color peppercorns

6 ounces cheese, such as Kefalo Graviera, cut into wedges

Coarse sea salt

Zest of 1 lemon

1 With a sharp knife, make a small cut lengthwise in the top of each date and remove the pit.

2 Lightly toast the almonds and walnuts in a small, dry nonstick skillet over medium-low heat. Using a teaspoon, fill the dates with the nut mixture.

3 Simmer the wine, honey, and pepper in a small saucepan over medium heat for about 15 minutes. Place the dates, cut side up, in the pan and continue to simmer until warm, about 5 minutes.

4 Serve the warm dates with the cheese wedges and top with a sprinkle of sea salt and lemon zest.

ORIGINAL RECIPE

Homemade sweet. Stone dates, and stuff with nuts, pine kernels, or ground pepper. Roll in salt, fry in cooked honey, and serve.

—ON COOKERY, APICIUS

MEDITERRANEAN FRUIT SALAD

Serves 12

A magnificent orchard stretches four acres deep. . . . Here luxuriant trees are always in their prime, pomegranates and pears, and apples glowing red, succulent figs . . . pear mellowing ripe on pear, apple on apple, cluster of grapes on cluster, fig crowding fig.

—HOMER, CIRCA 700 B.C.

This lovely passage about lush Sicily reminds me of the wonderful modern Italian fruit salad they call Macedonia. Italians claim the dish got its name because the country, like the fruit salad, is made up of many different parts. In fact, the key to this wonderful and refreshing salad is to combine lots of different fruit. I've included only what was available in antiquity, but if you like, you can add bananas, oranges, pineapple, and other fruits unknown to the ancient Greeks and Romans.

1 apple or pear, cored and diced

$\frac{1}{2}$ cup honey

8 ounces cherries, pitted

8 ounces grapes, sliced in half

4 apricots, pitted and diced

2 peaches, pitted and diced

2 plums, pitted and diced

1 pint raspberries or strawberries

1 pomegranate, seeds separated (optional)

3 figs, quartered

2 tablespoons sugar

$\frac{1}{4}$ cup fruit liqueur, such as limoncello

Toss the apple pieces in a large serving bowl with the honey to keep them from discoloring. Combine with the cherries, grapes, apricots, peaches, plums, and raspberries. Top with the pomegranate seeds, if using, and fig quarters. Sprinkle with the sugar and drizzle with the liqueur.

PEACHES IN SPICED WINE

Serves 4

Apicius, the first-century Roman gourmet, lists recipes for both peaches in wine and berries with vinegar in his Roman cookery book, proving that these favorite Italian summer desserts have a two-thousand-year-old tradition.

Originally from Persia, peaches were planted in ancient Greece and then introduced to the Romans. Initially, the Romans treated peaches with suspicion, believing that those picked in Persia were poisonous. Galen, the renowned second-century physician, even thought that peaches could cause fevers. Luckily for peach lovers, the Romans overcame their concerns and decided that peaches planted on Italian soil were safe.

3 firm peaches, peeled, pitted, and thinly sliced

2 tablespoons honey

1 cup dessert wine

1 teaspoon ground cumin

Divide the peach slices among 4 large wineglasses and top with the honey. Pour ¼ cup of the wine into each glass and sprinkle with the cumin. Serve immediately.

ORIGINAL RECIPE

A dish of peaches. Clean firm peaches, cut them into pieces, and boil. Arrange in a shallow pan, sprinkle with a little oil, and serve with cumin-wine sauce.

—*ON COOKERY*, APICIUS

MANY of the recipes in this chapter come from *On Cookery*, the first-century Roman cookbook hand-copied by monks in the ninth century. Only a few of the copies have survived; the oldest is housed in the New York Academy of Medicine Library in New York City.

Written on thick vellum by at least three different scribes, the 478 recipes are tightly consolidated into just fifty-seven pages—or, as scholars refer to them, "leaves." To economize on vellum, each recipe runs into the next without any clear demarcation, indent, or break.

It should not be surprising that a medical academy has an extensive collection of cookery books. Until this century almost all cookbooks contained numerous remedies and cures of various sorts, all of historic interest to medical professionals.

HAZEL-WALNUT HONEY CUSTARD

Serves 6

In ancient Rome, where walnuts were a child's favorite plaything, it was the custom to place baskets of them in the newlyweds' bedroom as a symbolic end of childhood.

Both children and adults will enjoy this nutty custard, from an ancient Roman cookbook, which can be made with ingredients that are probably already in your pantry. Toasting the crushed nuts before cooking not only increases the nutty flavor but also produces a no-fail, professional-looking golden top crust. Creamy and rich, this custard is an ideal dessert to serve when friends, young or old, drop by unexpectedly after dinner.

$1/4$ cup walnuts

$1/4$ cup blanched hazelnuts

2 cups whole milk

$1/4$ teaspoon ground nutmeg

Pinch of ground allspice

Pinch of freshly milled five-color peppercorns

$1/4$ cup plus 2 tablespoons honey

Pinch of salt

3 large eggs

1 large egg white

3 tablespoons nut liqueur, such as Frangelico or amaretto

1 Finely grind the walnuts and hazelnuts in a food processor. Toast the nut mixture in a small, dry nonstick skillet over medium heat for 2 to 3 minutes, until golden. Reserve 2 tablespoons.

2 Place the remaining toasted nuts and the milk, nutmeg, allspice, and pepper in a saucepan and bring to a low boil over medium-low heat. Gently simmer the mixture for 10 to 12 minutes to reduce the milk and infuse the flavors. Remove from the heat and stir in $1/4$ cup of the honey and the salt. Allow to cool to room temperature.

3 Preheat the oven to 325° F. Lightly grease six $1/2$-cup ramekins and place them in a deep baking pan.

4 In a small bowl, beat the eggs and egg white, then whisk them into the milk custard until well incorporated. Pour the custard into the ramekins. Fill the baking pan with hot water

until it reaches three-quarters of the way up the ramekins. Cover the pan with aluminum foil.

5 Bake in the center of the oven until set and firm, about 30 minutes. Turn off the heat but leave the ramekins in the oven for another 10 to 15 minutes.

6 While the custard is cooling in the oven, make the sauce. Mix the remaining 2 tablespoons of honey with the liqueur in a small bowl.

7 Serve the custards in the ramekins or, if you prefer, invert each onto a plate and then invert again onto a serving dish so that it rests golden side up. Drizzle with the honey-liqueur mixture and top with the reserved toasted nuts.

HONEY, the most important sweetener in antiquity, was valued for its ability to preserve foods. According to Aesop, a bee presented Zeus with a pot of honey as a gift. Zeus, pleased with the gesture, granted the bee a wish. The bee maliciously asked that its sting be fatal. To punish such a vindictive request, Zeus vowed that it would be the bee and not others who would die after stinging. And that, according to legend, is why to this day a bee dies if it loses its stinger.

BAY LEAF COOKIES
Makes 2½ dozen cookies

Grasp the subject, the words will follow.

—CATO THE ELDER, 234–149 B.C.

Daphne, a nymph, pleaded with Mother Earth for help in avoiding Apollo's amorous advances. Mother Earth obliged, changing her into a bay-laurel tree for protection. Zeus, watching the transformation, vowed to always wear a wreath of laurel leaves and make the laurel a part of all triumphal ceremonies in her memory.

Cato the Elder, the Roman statesman, inspired this memorable dish of bay leaf–flavored cookies.

8 tablespoons (1 stick) unsalted butter, at room temperature

½ cup plus 2 tablespoons sugar

1 large egg

¼ teaspoon salt

½ teaspoon baking soda

½ cup frozen white grape juice concentrate, thawed

1 teaspoon anise seeds

1 teaspoon ground cumin

2½ cups all-purpose flour

½ cup whole-milk ricotta cheese

3 bay leaves, finely crumbled and coated with olive oil

1 Preheat the oven to 350° F.

2 Beat the butter and ½ cup of the sugar in a large bowl using an electric mixer until creamy. Add the egg, salt, baking soda, grape juice concentrate, anise seeds, and cumin, and continue beating. Slowly add the flour until combined.

3 Drop the dough by rounded teaspoonfuls onto a greased nonstick cookie sheet and make an indent in the center of each with a teaspoon.

4 In a small bowl, mix together the cheese and remaining 2 tablespoons of sugar. Place half a teaspoonful of this sweet ricotta mixture in the center and top with a sprinkle of the crumbled bay leaves.

5 Bake on the center rack until the bottoms are golden brown, 15 to 18 minutes.

ORIGINAL RECIPE

Recipe for must [reduced pulp after the wine grapes are mashed] cake: Moisten 1 modius of wheat flour with must; add anise, cumin, 2 pounds of lard, 1 pound of cheese, and the bark of a laurel twig. When you have made them into cakes, put bay leaves under them, and bake.

— *ON AGRICULTURE*, CATO THE ELDER

AS A YOUTH in the military, Cato the Elder shared quarters with a soldier who introduced him to Pythagoras's philosophy for simple living and eating. As a result, Cato's dining habits changed. His breakfast, for example, "never saw the fire."

CANDY NUT CHEWS

Makes 2 pounds chews

Referred to as "the cake doctor" by ancient writers, Chrysippus is the author of a first-century B.C. Greek cookbook, *Bread-Making*. His book included recipes for many varieties of breads and desserts, such as cheese bread, spiced wine cake, pine nut cake, and these wonderful nut chews that Chrysippus said originated on the Greek island of Crete.

1 cup finely chopped walnuts

1 cup finely chopped blanched hazelnuts

1 cup finely chopped blanched almonds

$\frac{1}{2}$ cup sugar

2 cups honey

2 teaspoons freshly milled five-color peppercorns

1 tablespoon ground cardamom

$\frac{1}{4}$ cup sesame seeds

1   Preheat the oven to 350° F. Place the nuts on a nonstick baking sheet and bake until lightly toasted, 8 to 10 minutes.

2   Bring the sugar, honey, pepper, and cardamom to a boil in a large, heavy saucepan over medium heat. Cook until the mixture reaches 220° F on a candy thermometer.

3   Mix in the nuts and continue cooking, stirring frequently, for another 10 minutes, or until the candy pulls away from the sides of the pan and reaches 280° F. Remove from the heat.

4   Line a large nonstick baking sheet with parchment.

5   Using 2 well-greased teaspoons, drop the nut mixture onto the parchment 1 teaspoonful at a time, being careful not to touch the mixture because it is very hot. Allow 2 inches between the candies because they will spread as they cool.

6   Sprinkle with the sesame seeds and allow the chews to dry, about 30 minutes.

7   The chews can be stored on parchment paper in an airtight container for up to 2 weeks.

ORIGINAL RECIPE

In Crete, Chrysippus says, they make a small cake called gastris. It consists of the following: walnuts, hazelnuts, almonds, poppy-seed; roast them, tending them well, then mash them carefully in a clean mortar; having mixed the fruit with it, soften with boiled honey, adding considerable pepper, and soften; it becomes dark with the poppy-seed. Flatten it all out and make it into a square. Then mash some white sesame, soften it with boiled honey, and draw it out into two thin slabs, placing one below, the other on top of it in such a manner that the dark part comes in the middle, and shape it nicely. All this is from the wise cake-doctor, Chrysippus.

—"BREAD-MAKING," CHRYSIPPUS,
IN *THE PHILOSOPHER'S BANQUET*, ATHENAEUS

MILK AND HONEY
DESSERT TOASTS
Serves 4

Heaven's gift, honey from the skies.
—VIRGIL, 70–19 B.C.

Virgil, the first-century poet, wrote a book on bee-keeping. He lyrically described the best spot to place a hive: "Let clear springs be near, and moss-green pools, and a tiny brook stealing through the grass, and let a palm or huge wild olive shade." Virgil suggests that aromatic plants be grown near the hive, including "wild thyme with fragrance far born, and a wealth of strong scented savory; and let violet beds drink of the trickling spring."

This two-thousand-year-old Roman recipe for rich milk-and-honey-soaked bread, fried crisp and topped with spiced cherry wine, is wonderful for dessert or brunch. The secret is to use a crusty baguette and allow lots of time for it to soak up the milk and honey before cooking.

$3/_4$ cup red wine

4 whole cloves

One 2-inch cinnamon stick

$1/_4$ cup dried cherries

5 tablespoons honey

1 cup whole milk

1 large egg

8 baguette slices, 1 inch thick

2 tablespoons walnut or almond oil

Confectioners' sugar

1 Gently boil the wine, cloves, cinnamon, cherries, and 3 tablespoons of the honey in a small saucepan over medium heat until reduced by half, about 30 minutes. Remove the cloves and cinnamon stick, and discard. Reserve the wine syrup.

2 Beat together the remaining 2 tablespoons of honey, the milk, and the egg in a small bowl until well combined. Soak the bread slices in the milk mixture until all the liquid is absorbed, 3 to 4 minutes per side. Heat the oil in a large skillet over medium heat until hot but not smoking. Put the bread in the pan and cook until dark golden, about 2 minutes per side. Place the bread on absorbent paper to remove any excess oil.

3 Arrange the warm bread slices on a serving platter. Drizzle with the wine syrup and sprinkle with confectioners' sugar. Serve warm.

FIG GRANITA

Serves 4

Another thing we should note is the grace of Nature's processes. . . .
Figs at their ripest will crack open, which adds its own
particular beauty to the fruit.

—MARCUS AURELIUS, A.D. 121–180

Figs, thought to inspire pleasant dreams, were often eaten after dinner. Dried figs are sweet, long-lasting, and nutritious, so it's no wonder they were referred to as "that god-given inheritance of our mother country, darling of my heart." This lovely fig granita is easy to make and tastes even more delicious when topped with a dollop of mascarpone cheese or whipped cream.

1 cup white wine

$\frac{1}{2}$ pound whole dried figs, chopped

$\frac{1}{2}$ cup sugar

$\frac{1}{4}$ teaspoon ground ginger

1 tablespoon freshly squeezed lemon juice

$\frac{1}{4}$ cup mascarpone cheese or whipped cream

2 tablespoons minced candied ginger

1   Bring the wine to a boil in a large saucepan over medium-high heat. Cook until reduced by half, about 5 minutes. Add the figs, sugar, ginger, and 1 cup of water, and return to a boil. Lower the heat and simmer until the figs are very soft, about 10 minutes. Remove from the heat and allow to cool.

2   Transfer the mixture to a blender. Add the lemon juice and 1 cup of cold water, and puree until smooth. Pour the mixture into a shallow baking pan, cover with plastic wrap, and freeze for at least 4 hours.

3   Mash the mixture with a fork just before serving. Serve in chilled wineglasses with a dollop of the cheese topped with candied ginger.

ACCORDING to Greek myth, the goddess Demeter gave the fig tree and the secrets of its cultivation as a gift to a mortal who had shown her kindness.

WALNUT CAKE WITH FIG JAM
Serves 10 to 12

*There was a cake, my master, as big as this, and white; it was so thick that
it bulged from the basket, and when the cover was taken off, an odor and a
steam mingled with honey rose upward to the nostrils; for it was still hot.*

—NICOSTRATUS, CIRCA FOURTH CENTURY B.C.

This walnut cake with fig icing was originally baked as an offering to Iris, the goddess of rainbows. Made with both light and dark figs, this multilayered cake is quite delicious and, you guessed it, as beautiful as a rainbow.

In antiquity, cake studded with lights was offered to the goddess Artemis for the full moon celebration. Our custom of lighting candles on a birthday cake, in fact, dates to this ancient Greek practice.

1 cup sliced dried black figs

2 cups white wine

1 cup honey

1 cup sliced dried green figs

8 tablespoons (1 stick) unsalted butter, softened

1 cup sugar

6 large eggs, at room temperature, separated

2 cups all-purpose flour

2 teaspoons baking powder

$1/4$ teaspoon ground cinnamon

Pinch of ground cloves

Salt

$3/4$ cup whole milk

$1/4$ cup finely chopped walnuts

Confectioners' sugar

1   Simmer the black figs, 1 cup of the wine, and $\frac{1}{2}$ cup of the honey in a small saucepan until the figs are very soft, about 20 minutes. Allow to cool, then puree in a food processor. Reserve for the cake filling.

2   In another small saucepan, simmer the green figs, remaining 1 cup of wine, and remaining $\frac{1}{2}$ cup of honey until the figs are very soft, about 20 minutes. Allow to cool, then puree in a food processor. Reserve for icing the cake.

3   Preheat the oven to 350° F. Butter and flour a 10-inch springform pan.

4   Cream the butter and sugar together in a large bowl with an electric mixer until light and fluffy. Add the egg yolks, 1 at a time, mixing well after each addition.

5   In a small bowl, sift together the flour, baking powder, cinnamon, cloves, and a pinch of salt. Add to the butter mixture, alternating with the milk and mixing well between additions. Fold in the walnuts.

6   In a large bowl, using an electric mixer, beat the egg whites with a pinch of salt until they hold soft peaks. Using a large rubber spatula, mix about one-quarter of the whites into the batter to lighten it. Gently fold in the remaining whites until just incorporated. Pour into the prepared pan.

7   Bake for 35 to 40 minutes, or until a toothpick inserted in the center comes out clean. Allow the cake to cool completely on a rack.

8   Once the cake is cool, cut it horizontally into 2 layers using a serrated knife. Place the bottom layer on a serving plate and top with the dark fig filling. Place the top layer over the filling and glaze with the light fig icing. Dust with confectioners' sugar and serve.

PHYLLO-WRAPPED ALMOND SEMOLINA

Serves 8

The original Roman recipe was for spelt custard flavored with raisins, nuts, and sweet wine. In this modern version I have substituted light semolina to create a creamier custard and then wrapped it in classic phyllo dough and topped it with a delicious raisin-port syrup for an elegantly delicious reminder of the past.

$\frac{1}{2}$ cup sliced blanched almonds

3 cups whole milk

2 tablespoons sugar

2 tablespoons unsalted butter, plus melted butter for phyllo

$\frac{1}{2}$ teaspoon salt

$\frac{1}{2}$ cup plus 2 tablespoons semolina flour

2 cups port

$\frac{1}{3}$ cup golden raisins

3 tablespoons honey

1 package frozen phyllo dough, thawed

2 tablespoons confectioners' sugar

1   Preheat the oven to 350° F. To release the full flavor of the almonds, toast them on a non-stick baking sheet until light golden, about 5 minutes. Reserve 1 tablespoon for garnish. Put the rest in a food processor or spice mill and finely grind.

2   Combine the milk, sugar, butter, salt, and $\frac{1}{4}$ cup of finely ground almonds in a large saucepan and bring to a low boil over medium-low heat. Slowly add $\frac{1}{2}$ cup of semolina and stir constantly until the mixture thickens, 8 to 10 minutes. Put the pudding in a lightly greased 9 by 6-inch baking pan and refrigerate for at least 1 hour to set.

3   Meanwhile, bring the port, raisins, and honey to a boil in a small saucepan over medium heat. Simmer until the port is reduced by two-thirds, about 12 minutes. Set aside.

4   Cut the semolina pudding into 8 pieces.

5   Raise the oven heat to 375° F.

6 Unroll 1 sheet of phyllo dough and brush with melted butter. Sprinkle with a bit of the ground almonds and top with another sheet of phyllo dough. Brush that layer with butter and top with a third sheet. Cut these sheets in half. Put 1 piece of semolina pudding on each section and wrap like a package. Brush with butter. Put the wrapped bundles on a greased baking sheet, seam side down.

7 Repeat the procedure for the remaining 6 semolina pieces.

8 Bake until dark golden, about 20 minutes. Allow to cool slightly. Serve topped with a spoonful of the port sauce and a sprinkle of the confectioners' sugar and toasted sliced almonds.

THE ANCIENTS told time with sundials during the day. Water clocks, which measured time by the flow of water through a vessel, were used in the evening. Needless to say, clocks then were not precise, and reference to time was never incorporated into cooking directions. Chefs had to rely on the look and feel of food to know when it was done.

Not even the yearly calendar was uniform in antiquity. Depending on the country, the number of days per year ranged from 304 to 445. It wasn't until the reign of Julius Caesar, inspired by the Egyptians, that a standardized calendar was established. The Julian calendar, with its $365\frac{1}{4}$ days, was modified to our modern calendar of $364\frac{1}{4}$ days during the Renaissance.

Interestingly, the months of July and August were named after Roman emperors, Julius and Augustus Caesar. Various other rulers, including Nero, tried unsuccessfully to rename months after themselves. The Roman senate wanted to rename September after Emperor Tiberius, but he modestly vetoed the honor, wisely noting, "What will you do when there are thirteen Caesars?"

LAVENDER-HONEY APPLES IN PUFF PASTRY

Serves 4

As an apple reddens on the high bough; high atop the highest bough the apple pickers passed it by—no, not passed it by, but they could not reach it.

—SAPPHO, CIRCA 610—580 B.C.

Alexander the Great was so convinced of the healthful benefits of apples that he ate them at every meal.

The ancients regularly preserved fruit in honey, and you'll notice that when you coat apples with honey, they do not turn brown. Thanks to the many wonderful frozen puff pastry products on the market today, this tempting dessert is ready in minutes.

2 tablespoons honey

Pinch of dried lavender or dash of lavender water

4 small Red Delicious apples, peeled and cored

$\frac{1}{4}$ cup brown sugar

$\frac{1}{2}$ teaspoon ground nutmeg

$\frac{1}{2}$ teaspoon ground cinnamon

All-purpose flour for dusting

1 frozen puff pastry sheet, thawed

4 cinnamon sticks, long enough to peek out of the apples

1 large egg, well beaten

1   Preheat the oven to 400° F.

2   On a shallow plate, stir together the honey and lavender. Coat each apple with the scented honey.

3   In a small bowl, combine the brown sugar, nutmeg, and cinnamon. On a lightly floured work surface, roll the pastry sheet with a rolling pin into a 12-inch square and cut into 4 smaller squares. Roll the apples in the sugar mixture and place each one on a pastry square. Put a cinnamon stick in the center of each apple. Gather the edges of the pastry

together at the top of the apple and gently pinch together to help seal it. Brush the pastry with the egg and place the apples on a nonstick baking sheet.

4 Bake until golden, about 25 minutes.

APPLES were featured in many Greek and Roman myths. For example, according to legend one of Hercules' labors was to bring back the Golden Apples of the Hesperides. In another, Princess Atalanta, a swift-footed runner, placated her father, the king, by agreeing to marry. However, she would marry only a man who could beat her in a footrace. As Atalanta hoped, all her suitors lost the races against her. Ever on the side of love, Aphrodite finally intervened and gave one suitor magic apples to toss in Atalanta's path. The apples delayed her enough to allow the suitor to win the race and Atalanta's hand in marriage.

MINI RICOTTA FRITTERS

Makes 2 dozen mini puffs

This recipe by Cato the Elder, the second-century B.C. statesman, reminds me of the ricotta fritters traditionally sold at fairs in Italy. To avoid the mess of deep-frying I made the fritters bite-sized, which allows them to cook quickly in a small skillet in only a tiny bit of oil.

Topped with honey and poppy seeds, these ready-in-minutes fritters make a delicious dessert or unusual brunch.

1 cup whole-milk ricotta cheese

2 large eggs

2 tablespoons sugar

$\frac{1}{2}$ cup all-purpose flour

$\frac{1}{2}$ teaspoon salt

$\frac{1}{4}$ teaspoon baking soda

Vegetable oil for frying

2 tablespoons honey

1 tablespoon poppy seeds

1   Using an electric mixer, blend the cheese, eggs, and sugar in a large bowl until creamy. Slowly add the flour, salt, and baking soda, and blend until well combined.

2   Pour oil into a small nonstick frying pan to a depth of $\frac{1}{4}$ inch and heat over medium-low heat. Be sure the heat is not high, or the fritters will not puff up or cook through. Once the oil is warm, drop a teaspoonful of batter at a time into it. Cook, turning once, until both sides are golden.

3   Remove the fritters with a slotted spoon and place on absorbent paper or on a draining board.

4   Place the warm fritters on a serving platter, drizzle with the honey, and sprinkle with the poppy seeds. Serve immediately.

ORIGINAL RECIPE

Recipe for globi: Mix the cheese and spelt in the same way, sufficient to make the number desired. Pour lard into a hot copper vessel, and fry one or two at a time, turning them frequently with two rods, and remove when done. Spread with honey, sprinkle with poppy-seed, and serve.

—*ON AGRICULTURE*, CATO THE ELDER

HOMER'S words, written almost three thousand years ago, perfectly convey the joy of sharing a meal with friends. This chapter explores ancient dining customs and provides sample menus with hints on how to give your own Roman- or Greek- themed dinner, buffet, or party.

The social exchanges that occur over food and wine were as important to the ancients as they are to us today—important in creating and maintaining friendships and important in gaining an understanding of others through the exchange of ideas. As Plutarch, the first-century historian, observed, "A guest comes to share not only meat, wine, and dessert, but conversation, fun, and the amiability that leads to friendship." Plutarch goes on to add what all of us who have spent any time lingering over wine with friends intuitively know: "Drinking together does give men a chance to get some understanding of each other."

Chapter 9

MENUS AND ENTERTAINING

I myself feel that there is nothing more delightful than when the festive

mood reigns in the hearts of all the people and the banqueters listen to

a minstrel from their seats in the hall, while the tables before them

are laden with bread and meat, and a steward carries round the

wine he has drawn from the bowl and fills their cups.

This, to my way of thinking, is perfection.

—HOMER, *THE ODYSSEY*

Party Philosophy

What is more agreeable than one's home?

—CICERO, 106—43 B.C.

Dinner in antiquity was almost always a social affair shared with a few close friends at someone's home. Friendship, which Cicero said "unites human hearts," was strengthened over shared meals.

No matter how slapdash the plans, how simple the food, how disheveled the house, or how many chores are assigned to guests, eating with friends at home fosters an intimacy that is hard to imitate in a restaurant. As Homer stated in the *Odyssey*, "It's high time for a meal. I hope the men will be home at any moment so we can fix a tasty supper."

As a host, one of the first decisions you'll make is how many friends to invite. The ancients considered it ideal to have from three (the number of Graces) to nine (the number of Muses). For weddings and other important events, however, more than a hundred guests might be invited. The ideal number of guests was cause for much debate in antiquity. Some hosts speculated that a small number was preferable to avoid the embarrassment of running out of space or wine or food. Others, such as Plutarch, maintained, "If both space and the provisions are ample, we must still avoid great numbers, because they in themselves interfere with sociability and conversation."

Once you've settled on your guest list, the next step is to call or send invitations.

For small, informal dinner parties, the ancient Greek or Roman host extended a verbal invitation, usually during a workout at the public baths. For larger or more formal events, messengers delivered handwritten invitations. Several written on papyrus were discovered at the Alexandria library in Egypt. One wedding invitation from the third century reads, "Theon son of Origenes invites you to the wedding of his sister tomorrow, Tubi 9, at the 8th hour." My favorite, also from the third century, states, "Greeting, my lady Serenia, from Petosiris. Make every effort, dear lady, to come out on the 20th, the birthday festival of the god, and let me know whether you are coming by boat or by donkey, in order that we may send for you. Take care not to forget, dear lady. I pray for your lasting health."

The following samples of invitations can be copied in calligraphy or re-created on a computer. To give your invitation an authentic look, you might like to use papyrus or handmade rough paper that is available at specialty stationery shops. Or you might try staining ordinary paper with tea or wine. Burning or tearing the edges gives a whimsically aged effect. I like to close the envelopes with seals of Roman or Greek design, also available at stationery stores. Foreign stamps also make an unusual envelope decoration, so when I travel, I buy inexpensive postage stamps with interesting images. Seals with your initials and sealing wax of different colors can be purchased at fine stationery stores as well.

Sample Invitation 1

NEW YEAR'S EVE BACCHANAL

TURN BACK THE CLOCK 2,000 YEARS AND
RING IN THE NEW YEAR WITH AN ANCIENT ROMAN FEAST

FRUIT OF BACCHUS AND TIDBITS
INSPIRED BY ANCIENT ROMAN RECIPES

I dislike a drinking companion with a good memory.
—PLUTARCH, A.D. 46–120

NAME AND ADDRESS:

TIME:

DATE:

RSVP TO (PHONE NUMBER, NAME) BY (DATE)

Decadent Attire
(Togas Optional)

JOIN US ON NOVEMBER 7,

PLATO'S BIRTHDAY,

TO PONDER THE MEANING OF LIFE AND
SHARE IN EPICUREAN DELIGHTS

A good soul by its virtue
renders the body the best that is possible.
—PLATO

Astronomy compels the soul to look
upwards and leads us from this world to another.
—PLATO

Everything that deceives may be said to enchant.
—PLATO

Of all the animals,
the boy is the most unmanageable.
—PLATO

PLEASE COME TO THE HOME OF:

AT:

ON:

RSVP BY:

TO:

Sample Invitation 3

GREEK MYTH PARTY
COME AS YOUR FAVORITE GOD OR GODDESS!

AMBROSIA AND FESTIVITIES BEGIN

AT:

ON:

MUSIC

READINGS

RIDDLES OF THE SPHINX

MILD DEBAUCHERY

NAME:

ADDRESS:

RSVP TO:

BY:

Sample Invitation 4

OUTDOOR PICNIC AND
ZANY FAMILY OLYMPICS

FRISBEE DISCUS THROWING
ANT CHARIOT RACES
HOT DOG JAVELIN HURLING
THUMB WRESTLING

FOOD SERVED AT:
OLYMPICS BEGIN AT:

NAME:
ADDRESS:
DATE:
TIME:
RSVP BY:
TO:

Seating Philosophy

Interestingly, in antiquity the place of honor varied from country to country. For some it was the head of the table, and for others the central section. According to the first-century historian Plutarch, the seat of honor is for "the Persians the most central place, occupied by the king; the Greeks the first place; the Romans the last place on the middle couch."

A bad neighbor is a misfortune,
as much as a good one is a great blessing.
—HESIOD, CIRCA 800 B.C.

Not sure whether or not to set out place cards for your dinner party? Well, you are not alone. The ancients debated the issue, too. Plutarch, among others, discussed the philosophical merits of "whether the host should arrange the placing of his guests or leave it to the guests themselves."

Then, just as now, both assigning and not assigning seats had merit. Some ancients argued that seats should be assigned to give due respect to a guest's age and rank. They considered it rude not to assign persons of special status a place of honor or not to seat them near other important guests.

Others, also in favor of assigning seats, felt the decision should be based on who will get along rather than on rank: "For it is not prestige, but pleasure which must determine the placing of guests; it is not the rank of each which must be considered, but the affinity and suitability of each to each."

Still others argued, however, that the guests should decide for themselves where and with whom they were most comfortable sitting.

I usually opt for assigned seating, taking my cue from Hesiod, the ninth-century B.C. poet. He advised not to seat people in the same profession together, "for beggar is jealous of beggar and bard of bard." I also follow Plutarch's advice to "separate contentious, abusive, and quick-tempered men by placing between them some easygoing men as a cushion to soften their clashing" and match guests whose personality style and interests complement one another.

I approach seat assignments in much the same way I plan the flavor and texture balance of a menu. I would never serve mashed potatoes and pasta in the same course; they are too similar. Neither would I plate caviar with fried chicken, even though I adore both; they are too different. Very occasionally, though, I do pit rival flavors for an original zing. So, in theory, for lively dinner conversation be sure to keep pasta away from mashed potatoes and judiciously mix your caviar with fried chicken.

In creating the place cards I use materials that remind me of ancient Rome or Greece, such as travel or art postcards, torn sections of parchment paper, oyster shells, white marble fragments, and even large, smooth shards from broken terra-cotta planters. For variety I write a quote on one side of the place card and the guest's name on the back, and then everyone guesses where he or she is supposed to sit based on the quote. This method comes in handy if I need to buy a little extra time in the kitchen to get the first course ready.

Dining rooms in ancient Rome were richly decorated with frescoes, mosaics, and wall hangings. The floor was made festive with scattered flower petals. For your own Roman or Greek dinner party you might like to hang museum posters of ancient frescoes or mosaics. Scattered flower petals, both on the floor and on tabletops, are a lovely addition. I associate white marble with antiquity, so for my feasts I decorate the dining room with white draped cloth and any white or whitewashed terra-cotta pottery I find at tag sales and flea markets. Moss and fresh ivy are a nice touch, too. I buy small pots of them at the nursery and then give them to guests as party favors.

Epicurean Details

Pleasure is the beginning and the end of living happily.
—EPICURUS, 341–270 B.C.

Servants in antiquity ceremoniously washed guests' hands and offered them a drink as they entered the host's home. Homer mentioned this practice in 700 B.C.: "Heralds brought the water at once and rinsed their hands, and the young men brimmed the mixing bowls with wine, and tipping first drops for the gods in every cup, they poured full rounds for all."

Although we no longer wash our guests' hands, we do offer our guests a drink as soon as they arrive, just as was done then.

The wine urges me on, the bewitching wine, which sets even
a wise man to singing and to laughing gently and rouses him up
to dance and brings forth words which were better unspoken.
—HOMER, *THE ODYSSEY*

In antiquity, wine was drunk diluted, and it was up to the host's discretion to determine the ratio of water to wine, the size of the wine cups, and how many rounds of wine would be served, the norm being a fifty-fifty ratio with three rounds. Socrates, a frequent guest at symposia, was noted as being in favor of "small cups sprinkled frequently, so that we will be seduced into reaching a state of amusement, instead of being forced by the wine into drunkenness." Apparently, however, drunkenness was often a consequence, as there are many ancient remedies for hangovers.

Wine grapes have been cultivated in the Mediterranean region since antiquity, so any type of red or white wine is perfectly authentic for your antiquity-themed dinner party. You might like to serve retsina, a classic Greek wine, or wines from Sicily, one of Italy's first wine-producing regions. I like the Sicilian wines Mamertino, Sangiovese, Corvo, and Eloro. Be sure to try one of the many wonderful dessert wines with your sweets course, as was done in antiquity. My favorites include the Italian dessert wines Vino Santo, Moscato d'Siracusa, and Marsala, and the Greek dessert wines Samos and Mavrodaphne.

The Philosophy of Conversation

Do not invite either too talkative or too silent guests,
since eloquence is appropriate to the Forum and the courts,
and silence to the bedroom, but neither to a dinner.

—MARCUS VARRO, 116—27 B.C.

The ancients appreciated good conversationalists and offered advice on how to improve one's skills. Plutarch, writing in the first century, suggested that asking questions on a topic someone knows well will spark interesting conversation: "Thus travelers and sailors are very glad to be questioned about a far-away place and a foreign sea and about the customs and laws of alien men." Varro, who wrote a book of humorous essays on vice, advised that conversation should be "diverting and cheerful," and we should "talk about matters which relate to the common experience of life."

Jokes and storytelling were then, as now, a lively part of dinner conversation, and certain guests were invited to dinner because of their wit. Said one guest at Xenophon's banquet, "The reason I got invitations to dinner was that I might stir up laughter among the guests and make them merry." Advice on not only how to tell a good joke but also on how to avoid inadvertently offending a fellow guest was offered by Plato and others. Plato contended that to "joke with grace and good taste is a task for the well-educated man." Two thousand years ago, Plutarch counseled that "the man who cannot engage in joking at a suitable time, discreetly and skillfully, must avoid jokes altogether" and that humor should be "casual and spontaneous, not brought in from a distance like previously prepared entertainment." This still sounds like good advice today.

I loved reading about the ancients' dinners. Plutarch mentioned dinner conversations about such far-flung topics as "whether the hen or the egg came first" and "whether the sea is richer in delicacies than the land." Another topic weighed the health merits of eating a wide variety of foods. For Plutarch, "variety is more agreeable, and . . . the more agreeable is the more appetizing, and the more appetizing is the more healthful."

To spark animated discussions at my dinner table, besides seating fried chicken next to caviar, I distribute controversial quotes from antiquity such as these:

Extreme right is extreme wrong.
—CICERO, 106—43 B.C.

We make war that we may live in peace.
—ARISTOTLE, 384—322 B.C.

There is no animal more invincible than a woman,
nor fire either, nor any wildcat so ruthless.
—ARISTOPHANES, 450—388 B.C.

Great friends and good conversation deserve wonderful food. The ancient Greeks and Romans served guests either individual plated portions or from communal platters, family style. The merit of each was fodder for philosophical discussion. Plutarch believed that individual portions "kills sociability" because it reduces the chance for conversation that comes with passing food family style. Since I enjoy variety, for sit-down dinners I opt for a combination of both, serving the appetizer and dessert courses already plated and the main course communally. I plate the appetizers and dessert before guests arrive so that I have less rushing around to do at the start and end of the meal.

Following are five suggested menus for sit-down dinners, buffets, and outdoor parties.

Mix stronger wine. A cup for the hands of each guest—
here beneath my roof are the men I love the most.
—HOMER, *THE ILIAD*

It is my hope that through this book you will feel connected to the past in a new way and be inspired to host your own feasts so that those you love will linger at your table for long hours.

Fall Dinner Party Menu

APPETIZERS
Herbed Olive Puree, page 5
Assorted Cheeses
Pepper Twists, page 179

FIRST COURSE
Arugula and Radicchio with Ginger-Date Vinaigrette, page 67

MAIN COURSE
Marjoram Chicken, page 140
Herbed Barley with Pancetta, page 47
Roasted Leeks and Apple, page 82

DESSERT
Walnut Cake with Fig Jam, page 216
Candy Nut Chews, page 210

▣ ▣ ▣

Winter Buffet Menu

BUFFET
Seared Sirloin with Lemon-Herb Crème Fraîche, page 10
Shrimp with Aromatic Herbs, page 99
Chicken from Ancient Africa, page 143
Kale with Coriander Sauce, page 74
Poppy Turnips for King Nicomedes, page 87
Etruscan Focaccia, page 189

DESSERT
Mini Ricotta Fritters, page 223
Hazel-Walnut Honey Custard, page 205

Spring Menu

APPETIZERS
Lamb on Skewers with Mint Marmalade, page 15
Asparagus Frittata, page 21

FIRST COURSE
Spring Pea and Fennel Puree, page 59

MAIN COURSE
Red Snapper in Parchment, page 93
Golden Chickpea Circles, page 89
Oven-Roasted String Beans, page 75

DESSERT
Mediterranean Fruit Salad, page 200
Milk and Honey Dessert Toasts, page 212

Outdoor Summer Party

BUFFET
Free-Form Cherry Lasagna, page 27
Grapes-and-Couscous-Stuffed Chicken Breasts, page 137
Assorted Grilled Meats with Seasoned Salt, page 169
Marinated Chicken with Date Mustard, page 128
Baby Greens with Caper Vinaigrette, page 66
Grilled Celery with Anchovy-Lemon Sauce, page 81
Barley Rolls of Lesbos, page 182

DESSERT
Fig Granita, page 215
Peaches in Spiced Wine, page 201

Vegetarian Feast

FIRST COURSE

Red Lentils in Garlic-Roasted Artichoke Bottoms, page 19
Pea Soufflé with Fresh Dill, page 85

MAIN COURSE

Spaghetti with Caramelized Onions, page 13
Field and Forest Salad, page 71
Crisp Chickpea Wedges, page 174

DESSERT

Bay Leaf Cookies, page 207
Dates in Spiced Wine, page 199

SELECTED BIBLIOGRAPHY

Translated ancient texts

Apicius. *Cookery and Dining in Imperial Rome.* Edited and translated by Joseph Dommers Vehling. New York: Dover Publications, 1977.

Apicius. *The Roman Cookery Book.* Translated by Barbara Flower and Elisabeth A. Rosenbaum. London: George G. Harrap, 1958.

Aristotle. *The Basic Works of Aristotle.* Edited by Richard McKeon. New York: Modern Library, 2001.

Athenaeus. *The Deipnosophists,* books 1–15 (*The Philosopher's Banquet*). Translated by C. B. Gulick. Cambridge, Mass.: Harvard University Press, 1929.

Cato. *On Agriculture.* In Cato and Varro, *On Agriculture.* Translated by W. D. Hooper. Rev. by H. B. Ash. Cambridge, Mass.: Harvard University Press, 1935.

Cicero. Marcus Tullius. *On the Good Life.* Translated by Michael Grant. London: Penguin Books, 1971.

Galen. *On Food and Diet.* Translated by Michael Grant. London: Routledge, 2000.

Galen. *On the Natural Faculties.* Translated by A. J. Brock. Cambridge, Mass.: Harvard University Press, 1916.

Gellius, Aulus. *Attic Nights,* books 1–20. Translated by J. C. Rolfe. Cambridge, Mass.: Harvard University Press, 1927.

Hippocrates. vols. 2 and 4. Translated by W.H.S. Jones. Cambridge, Mass.: Harvard University Press, 1923.

Homer. *The Iliad.* Translated by Robert Fagles. New York: Penguin Books, 1998.

Homer. *The Odyssey.* Translated by Robert Fagles. New York: Penguin Books, 1998.

Juvenal and Persius. Translated by G. G. Ramsay. Cambridge, Mass.: Harvard University Press, 1918.

Marcus Aurelius. *Meditations.* Translated by Maxwell Staniforth. London: Penguin Books, 1964.

Martial. *Epigrams.* Translated by J. Michie. New York: Modern Library, 1972.

Petronius. *The Satyricon*, 2nd ed. Translated by J. M. Mitchell. London: George Routledge and Sons; New York: E. P. Dutton, 1923.

Pliny. *Natural History.* Translated by H. Rackham, W.H.S. Jones, and D. E. Eichholz. Cambridge, Mass.: Harvard University Press, 1962.

Plutarch. *Lives,* vols. 1 and 2. Translated by John Dryden. New York: Modern Library, 2001.

Plutarch. *Moralia.* Translated by Paul A. Clement and Herbert B. Hoffleti. Cambridge, Mass.: Harvard University Press, 1969.

Select Papyri, Non-Literary Papyri, Private Affairs. Translated by A. S. Hunt and C. C. Edgar. Cambridge, Mass.: Harvard University Press, 1932.

Select Papyri, Poetry. Translated by D. L. Page. Cambridge, Mass.: Harvard University Press, 1941.

Suetonius. *The Twelve Caesars.* Translated by Robert Graves. Middlesex and New York: Penguin Books, 1979.

Tacitus. *The Histories.* Translated by W. H. Fyfe. Rev. and ed. by D. S. Levene. Oxford and New York: Oxford University Press, 1997.

Varro. *On Agriculture.* In Cato and Varro, *On Agriculture.* Translated by W. D. Hooper. Rev. by H. B. Ash. Cambridge, Mass.: Harvard University Press, 1935.

Virgil, Eclogues, Georgics, and Aeneid, 1–6. Translated by H. R. Fairclough. Rev. by G. P. Goold. Cambridge, Mass.: Harvard University Press, 2001.

Xenophon, 7 vols. Translated by E. C. Marchant and O. J Todd. Cambridge, Mass.: Harvard University Press, 1923.

INDEX

ABOUT THE AUTHOR

Noted psychologist, food historian, and cooking enthusiast
Francine Segan has appeared on numerous television
programs, including *Today*, Food Network's Top Five,
Regis Philbin, and Fox News, as well as WABC and
NPR radio. She lectures on food history at Marymount
College and the 92nd Street Y, and for various universities,
museums, historic homes, and theater festivals. Along
with her husband, Marc, and two children, Samantha and
Max, Segan divides her time between New York City, Italy,
and the Berkshires. She is the author of *Movie Menus* and
Shakespeare's Kitchen, both published by Random House.

ABOUT THE PHOTOGRAPHER

Tim Turner, winner of the 1999 and 2001 James Beard
Best Food Photography Award, has collaborated on more
than twenty bestselling cookbooks, including *Kitchen
Sessions with Charlie Trotter*, Jacques Pepin's *Sweet
Simplicity*, *Weber's Art of the Grill*, and *The Inn at Little
Washington*. He has also received many IACP, Clio, and
Addy awards and nominations for his work. Turner lives
in Chicago with his wife and three daughters.

ABOUT THE TYPE

The text of this book was set in Filosofia. It was designed in 1996 by Zuzana Licko, who created it for digital typesetting as an interpretation of the sixteenth-century typeface Bodoni. Filosofia, an example of Licko's unusual font designs, has classical proportions with a strong vertical feeling, softened by rounded droplike serifs. She has designed many typefaces and is the cofounder of *Emigre* magazine, where many of them first appeared. Born in Bratislava, Czechoslovakia, Licko came to the United States in 1968. She studied graphic communications at the University of California at Berkeley, graduating in 1984.